The Secret Symmetry of Mai and Freud

The Secret Symmetry of Maimonides and Freud presents the parallels between *The Guide of the Perplexed* and *The Interpretation of Dreams*, considering how Maimonides might be perceived as anticipating Freud's much later work.

The Secret Symmetry of Maimonides and Freud suggests that humankind has secrets to hide and does so by using common mechanisms and embedding revealing hints for the benefit of the true reader. Using a psychoanalytic approach in tandem with literary criticism and an in-depth assessment of Judaica, Szajnberg demonstrates the similarities between these two towering Jewish intellectual pillars. Using concepts of esoteric literature from the Torah and later texts, this book analyses their ideas on concealing and revealing to gain a renewed perspective on Freud's view of dreams. Throughout, Szajnberg articulates the challenges of reading translated works and how we can address the pitfalls in such translations.

The book is a vital read for psychoanalysts in training and practice, as well as those interested in Judaica, the history of ideas, and early medieval studies.

Nathan Szajnberg is a training analyst and retired Sigmund Freud Professor of Psychoanalysis at The Hebrew University, Israel. Szajnberg was born in Germany, grew up in Rochester, NY, and attended the College and Medical School at the University of Chicago, USA. His residencies include pediatrics, general, and child psychiatry, and he completed his psychoanalytic training at the St. Louis Institute, USA. He lives in Palo Alto with his wife and four children.

"Once one starts reading one wonders at the depth and meaning of the connection between these two wise souls. They enrich and add to each other across seven hundred years, bringing to light how past and present interact, opening dimensions and possibilities of being in our ongoing search and growth. A stimulating and healing contribution that keeps giving, at once awakening and restoring."

Michael Eigen, author of *The Challenge of Being Human, Contact with the Depths*, and *Faith*.

"Nathan Szajnberg has recognized a stunning link between 12th century Physician-Rabbi and a 19-20th century physician-psychologist. Each one found the cipher that aids understanding of esoteric narratives that enhance our lives. The story of discovery was a task of a lifetime revealing Szajnberg's genius: seeing connections across his career and across centuries. The volume exposes another connection among the three that represents the revival of Aristotilean thought that promotes the cultivation of Reason. A great story for anyone who loves scholarship!"

Theodore Shapiro, MD, Emeritus Professor, Weill Cornell Medicine. Editor Jnl. American Psychoanalytic Assoc. (1983–1992)

"Studying Freud—particularly in some key chapters of the "Interpretation of Dreams"—is not easy reading, but it is enriching reading. This work in particular requires that we re-read every page, sometimes even every paragraph in order to fully grasp the depth of what Freud reveals about the workings of the mind through his understanding of the dream work and of the importance of discovering that which is hidden in the dream in order to better understand ourselves. This is, of course, also very true of reading Maimonides "Mishneh Torah" and "Guide" as the close study of these texts allows the reader to grasp hidden meanings that can enlighten, just as the interpretation of a dream can inform the dreamer of that which was hitherto unknown. This scholarly and well-referenced book is also about studying and not just reading; every page gives us new facts, makes new connections, and brings to light hidden connections, mechanisms and associations, thus showing a continuity in mental processes from the past to the present. Nathan Szajnberg takes us on a distinctive voyage of discovery; by the end of his book, the reader is left with a sense of awe and pleasure at how much has been learned."

Dr Edward Nersessian, Training and supervising psychoanalyst at New York Psychoanalytic Institute, Clinical Professor of Psychiatry, Weill Cornell Medical College, Director for The Helix Center for Multidisciplinary Studies

"Szajnberg has a brilliant talent for exposing latent relationships between Freud's dream theory and Jewish mysticism. He shows Maimonides as a brilliant dialectician whose use of simile and metaphor exposed latent relationships. Following the author's integrative expository talent is an exposure to wisdom and an intellectual treat"

Peter Loewenberg, Professor Emeritus, UCLA

The Secret Symmetry of Maimonides and Freud

Nathan Szajnberg

Routledge
Taylor & Francis Group

LONDON AND NEW YORK

Designed cover image: Carlos Sanchez as rendered the owner of the image on Getty Images.

First published 2023

by Routledge
4 Park Square, Milton Park, Abingdon, Oxon OX14 4RN

and by Routledge
605 Third Avenue, New York, NY 10158

Routledge is an imprint of the Taylor & Francis Group, an informa business

© 2023 Nathan Szajnberg

British Library Cataloguing-in-Publication Data
A catalogue record for this book is available from the British Library

ISBN: 978-1-032-41466-9 (hbk)
ISBN: 978-1-032-41465-2 (pbk)
ISBN: 978-1-003-35821-3 (ebk)

DOI: 10.4324/9781003358213

Typeset in Times New Roman
by KnowledgeWorks Global Ltd.

To my children Nathan, Yadid, Uriel, and
Magnolia Ester., Sonia Aviva and Lily and
to Yikun, *eishat chayil.* To Peter Giovacchini
and Robert Michels, my two Virgils. And to
the University of Chicago, which provided an
intellectual refuge with dedicated teachers.

Contents

Acknowledgments

Working with Maimonides' *Guide* meant depending upon the great work translated by Shlomo Pines along with Leo Strauss and Ralph Lerner. But to weigh the meanings of specific words and phrases means relying on the Hebrew translation by ibn Tibbon, approved by Maimonides, and the original Judeo-Arabic. For this, I relied upon Myron Joshua, Josef Stern, and Daniel Birnstiel. Stern (University of Chicago) helped with "parable" and careful translations from Judeo-Arabic and Medieval Hebrew; Birnstiel (Senior Research Fellow, Institute for the Study of Islamic Culture and Religion, Goethe University) helped with his knowledge of Judeo-Arabic and ancient Semitic languages.

Much of this thinking was initiated by Chaim Belmaker's invitation to me twice as Visiting Professor at Ben Gurion University, where I first began to think about Joseph's dreams (in Hebrew).

Prior to that was the University of Chicago's foundation for me as an intellectual home, particularly to Mr. Bellow, who walked me home after a Joyce class; for Mr. Rago, who walked me around the Quadrangle to talk when I could think of a paper topic and I realized it would be comparing Job and Lear as tragic characters. And, of course, to Bruno Bettelheim, who awakened an understanding of psychoanalysis when I was 17 and he later remained dedicated to becoming a better psychoanalyst (and person).

Preface

Rambam and Freud: A Secret Symmetry

A personal history of how this book began some five decades ago, then developed as part of a University course, then a book on Western literature and its developing representations of inner life.

This book began some six decades ago in a failed endeavor. I was a student at the University of Chicago in the New Collegiate Division, the undergraduate version of the Committee on Social Thought. Teachers in the NCD included Jamie Redfield, Henry Rago, Jonathan Z. Smith, Herman Sinaiko, and Saul Bellow. My major was initially History and Philosophy of Religion, then after Mr. Rago's too premature death at 56,[1] I was switched to History of Religions with Jonathan Z. Smith (shadowed by the elusive Mircea Eliade haunting the fringes of campus). We were required to write a bachelor's thesis for graduation from NCD. My proposal was a study of Maimonides' (Rambam) *Guide of the Perplexed.* My mentor was Ralph Lerner, who (I did not realize this at first) assisted Shlomo Pines and Leo Strauss in the landmark English translation of the *Guide* from Judaio/Arabic.

My proposal was accepted. Mr. Lerner sent me at the start of the summer a single-spaced, two-sided page of readings ... in Hebrew, Arabic, Greek, and Latin, a smattering of English. I spent the broiling, humid summer in Chicago chasing down the English books listed, traveling to Northwestern's un-air-conditioned library for some books not found at Chicago's new Regenstein Library. I had known that most NCD students took 5–6 years, even seven to finish their theses. Wayne Booth once extolled the NCD BA theses as more alive and compelling than some Ph.D. theses. But, as an immigrant whose father was a factory machinist, I, on a hefty scholarship, could not afford 5–8 years for a BA.

At summer's end, during the *yamim ha'no'raim*, the "terrible days" between Rosh Hashannah and Yom Kippur, I approached Mr. Lerner, who was leaning against the white-enameled wooden kitchen cupboards at Hillel House, and confessed to him that I did not know Arabic, Greek nor Latin. (I was too embarrassed to confess my modest Hebrew.) He, with soft brown consoling eyes, responded, seeking to reassure me, "That's alright. You'll learn."

Then, I knew I had to decamp to medical school. I stayed in Chicago, but skipped across 58th Street to embark on my decades-long medical career.

In 2010, after three years as the Sigmund Freud Professor at the Hebrew University,[2] I returned to the United States. In Israel, I taught a course on literature and inner development for three years, based on Auerbach's *Mimesis*, catalyzed by a course with Mr Bellow on Joyce's *Ulysses* decades earlier. While completing a book summarizing the major trends in the representation of inner development in Western literature, Maimonides returned to haunt me. (The reader will see I remain anchored at the University of Chicago intellectually.) I kept returning to Leo Strauss's lectures on Maimonides, particularly enchanted by the found audiotape of his 1964 Hillel House lecture that became his introduction to the Pines translation. Now, some decades later as a psychoanalyst, I heard Maimonides—I prefer "Rambam"— in a new voice. In Strauss's terms, there is a genre of *esoteric* narrative—the voice of the hidden, yet also revealed—to which Rambam (and in his view, Bible) belongs.

Of course, the reader will gather in the course of this book, psychoanalysis, particularly the study of dreams, belongs to this "genre" of esoteric narrative. I shift from "literature" to "narrative" as both Rambam and Freud (and others from Torah, Socrates, and Christ) emphasized the power of oral-aural transmission over writing. Strauss led me to Halbertal, Josef Stern, and others. Robert Alter's meticulous attention to the Hebrew translation of the Torah supported my flaneur-like meanderings through Torah and Rambam.

What struck me and what I will explore, develop, and articulate in this book is the compelling continuity of specific mental mechanisms not only from Rambam through Freud but also reaching back to Torah, New Testament, and Socrates. That is, as Strauss (1963) and later Halbertal (2014) put it, there is a literature/narrative of the hidden and revealed. And a key to this genre is that the art of hiding includes the hints to how to *reveal* its richer, secret meanings, often only to the "elect," those trained to discover the keys to these word-treasure chests.

In this book, I will explicate that Rambam's insights into the esoteric— into the techniques to hide and also to reveal what's hidden— capture *mechanisms of the human mind* that later resonated in Freud's work on dream construction and subsequent interpretation. I will give an overview of what we know of Rambam's life and how this casts light on his decision to write his "mysterious" (Strauss) book, particularly the drowning death of his only brother. Then, I shift to his youthful, monumental *Mishnah Torah (MT)*, extolled by many even contemporary Orthodox Jews and even studied daily.

I will try to show that the *MT*, apparently an exoteric book on commandments, contains within it seeds of esoterism.

The chapter on the *Guide* will study Rambam's explicit alleged aims of his *Guide*. Then we hear his contradictory statements about its aims. Then we learn his explicit "guide" to the *techniques of hiddenness* he uses, such as contradictions, omissions, additions, and parables (which at first he states he won't use) with parallels to the Biblical techniques of parable and metaphor. Rambam's unique definition of "parable" (Stern, 2014) complements his techniques of concealing/revealing and points to Freud's idea of the dream's "navel."

This leads us to examine Freud's account of our inner three techniques of hiding meanings within our dreams, what Freud calls "dream work." And Freud's greater contribution: once we understand our techniques for hiding meaning from ourselves, we can unravel the knots of meanings within our dreams and reveal ourselves to ourselves.

The final chapter is an overview of mental life and how it remains the same over eons, even as we get greater access to its meaning, its techniques, and its embedded wisdom.

I close this preface with a childhood connection to Maimonides/Rambam and the bivalent charge he represented in my childhood Orthodox community. Once, on Rochester's Monroe Avenue, cars whizzing by, on a Shabbat Yom Kippur fast, we, a bevy of Orthodox buddies in our early teens, waited for the light to change for our crossing. At the red light, we examined each other's tongues for the milky white coating that proved our fasting. Two were cousins and only-children, Joe and Johnny. They were a Mutt and Jeff pair—one towering, slouching forward, the other diminutive, always peering, neck-craning upward. Joe whispered to us that he would show how his cousin didn't know that Rambam and Maimonides were the same. He asked Johnny, "So, what do you think of Rambam?" And Johnny responded with adulation. Then, he asked Johnny about Maimonides, to which Johnny responded with a spitting "*Apikoires*! *Apikoires*!" (Literally, Epicurean; figuratively, an apostate). We guffawed, and then explained to Johnny that they were one and the same man. The writer of the *Mishnah Torah* (taught reverently) later wrote the *Guide* (not taught, to our knowledge at all in Yeshivas). In fact, the *Guide* was banned in parts of Provence and Spain shortly after Rambam's death. This vignette captures the ongoing ambivalent status that Rambam/Maimonides had and continues to have.

Here, let us turn to the medieval "*Apikoires*" who was also the revered rabbi and how he unveiled his knowledge of inner life's concealed/revealed mechanisms. But we do this following my path of discovery—from Freud, a modern "*Apikoires*," pirouetting via Strauss to leap backward in time some nine centuries to Rambam/Maimonides.

Notes

1 This was shortly after the tumultuous "sit-in" at Chicago (and elsewhere) that ultimately was destructive to the College. Likely a heartbreaking event for Mr. Rago, a dedicated teacher in the College who accommodated our sit-in

by teaching outside, beneath an oak tree. For an account from a sympathetic faculty member, see Wayne Booth's *Now Don't Try to Reason with Me*, whose title captures many students' self-defeating state of mind during this episode (University of Chicago Press).

2 I am deeply grateful to Chaim Belmaker, Ret. Prof of Psychiatry, for inviting me twice as Visiting Professor at Ben Gurion University (during the Second Intifada), then recommending me to the President of the Hebrew University for the Freud Chair.

References

Halbertal, M. (2014). *Maimonides' Life and Thought*. Princeton.

Stern, J. (2014). *Matter and Form in Maimonides' Guide*. Harvard

Strauss, L. (1963). How to begin to Study The Guide of the Perplexed. In *Leo Strauss on Maimonides*. U of Chicago Press, pp. 417–490.

Chapter 1

Introduction—Maimonides' *Guide of the Perplexed* as a Medieval Precursor to Freud's *Interpretation of Dreams*

This book reaches back to medieval wisdom literature (Bloom, 2004) to find an account that presages Freud's view of Unconscious/Preconscious techniques of dream work. We argue that Maimonides presaged Freud, not that Freud read Maimonides, nor a continuity from Maimonides to Freud. Rather, we argue for analogies. Aristotle described man as a hopper, leaping to reach the heavens then brought back to earth by gravity (Klein, 1968). Occasional geniuses like Maimonides or Freud reach the "heavens" of understanding inner life; we aspire to what they learn as they limn the heavens of inner life.

We describe four prescient descriptions of "mental" mechanisms for hiding/revealing by Maimonides of *Torah* text—prescient of Freud's account of dream work.[1]

These are as follows:

1 An emotionally important narrative text (*Torah*/dream) has both latent and manifest meanings.
2 Oral recounting is the best method to uncover hidden meanings, although one "settles" for written recounting to preserve ideas.
3 There is a logic to hiding manifest texts, which contain revealing hints *for those well-trained.*
4 What is hidden is unacceptable to the reader/dreamer *and even to society, which would reject, even excommunicate the revealer.* For the dreamer, "excommunication" involves repression, suppression, or splitting off. For Freud, the writer, revealing the unacceptable risked alienation, even social excommunication by society and his colleagues.

Maimonides describes the following four pathways of concealment/revelation parallel to dream work:

1 *The visual* (in *Torah*) *hides the word* which *hides the abstract concept.*
2 We can discover the content hidden within the text.

DOI: 10.4324/9781003358213-1

3   Maimonides *wrote* the *Guide* meticulously in order to confound, using specific techniques (later mirrored dream work). Maimonides' intent was *to hide* from most readers, *yet reveal* to those most scholarly the secrets of his work, which in turn reveal the secrets of the *Torah*. Maimonides, so to speak, used "defense mechanisms" to protect himself *and* the reader.

4   And, significantly, a fundamental underlying principle of *Torah* that parallels Freud's view of dreams/inner life is that there are layers from manifest "text" to deeper, more hidden, and more meaningful latent "text." But first, an abbreviated recounting of Freud's dream work will help us see the remarkable parallels to Maimonides. Dream work "transforms the latent dream-thoughts into the manifest dream" (Auchinclass and Samberg, 2012). In his topographic model, Freud attributes to the Ucs. archaic primary process thinking, which produces wishes and fantasies striving for satisfaction but repressed during waking life.

Three types of dream regression facilitate dream formation:

1   *Topographic* "towards the sensory … reaching the perceptual …" (Freud, 1900)
2   *Formal*, primitive, particularly visual methods of representation
3   *Temporal* to older psychic structures, particularly early memories

And the primary process as manifested in dream work consists of the following three types:

1   *Condensation* (ideas/images compressed)
2   *Displacement* (one thing substituted for another)
3   Symbolic *representation* (Ucs. image substitution)

We emphasize this important parallel to the *Guide*: "these *mechanisms* … *disguise and distort the original unconscious dream-thoughts and wishes*" (Auchinclass and Samberg, 2012, p. 64).

An additional (fourth) technique of repressibility (an abstract idea represented by a concrete pictorial image) is that dream formation is influenced by secondary revision (elaboration), which is influenced by the secondary process and rearranges the dream, so it feels more logical. The Preconscious and Conscious Systems work on the dream to make it more linear/plausible.[2]

We recall Freud's Irma dream as a paradigm of dream content and the work it entailed and dream interpretation and its work. Blechner (2013) summarizes post-Freud development of ideas about dreams. This goes beyond this book. The basic ideas remain fundamentally the same: "impose *waking meaning* on *sleeping thought*" (Stimmel in Blechner, 2013).

This book's primary approach is comparing Maimonides's account (of the "work" of the *Torah and* his *Guide*) with Freud's description of dream work. We will review allusions to techniques (Maimonides' and Freud's) for unraveling what is hidden in both texts. In fact, Maimonides uses the Hebrew *histir*—hidden or secret—for content in both *Torah* and the *Guide*. In this analogy, Freud's dreams are like Maimonides' *Torah*: Freud's interpretative techniques are like the *Guide*. This is paradoxical for Maimonides, who *both conceals*, yet also offers techniques to *reveal* the hidden truths. Maimonides, we might say, is doing "textual" analysis, a form of analytic explication pre-Freud.

Dreams are a version of "secret" communication (to ourselves and, if spoken, to others).[3] The nature of secrets and secrecy is that tension is built into them (Szajnberg, 1992). Unlike privacy (which lacks this tension), "... the secret is something held *and withheld*; the secret hints at both its value and that it can be revealed ... but only to the proper or deserving audience" (Szajnberg, ibid.). Like the sacred (versus the profane), the secret is precious ground and differs from the mundane (Durkheim, 1987; Eiliade, 1987). Only valuables are kept hidden or secret, such as the family jewels. Maimonides' thesis is: while much of the *Torah* is overtly understandable (e.g., the Ten Commandments), there are precious jewels embedded within the *Torah*. Further—bringing us closer to Freud's dream book— Maimonides knew that if he were to overtly reveal the hidden secrets of the *Torah*, he risked excommunication.[4] (There is a long tradition of esoteric secrets in parables—Christ's "I have yet many things to say to you, but *you cannot bear them now*" (John 16:12) through Galileo's writing in mirror script, up to Freud and the present.) Therefore, Maimonides wrote the *Guide* esoterically, using parables, metaphors and at least six types of contradictions in order to both conceal and reveal the secrets within.[5] Like Freud, Maimonides offered techniques to guide us to understanding our nether world, embedded within *Torah*/dreams.[6]

One reason to study Maimonides' *Guide* is that it contains wisdom of the human soul, at least the wisdom of a twelfth-century genius. Is this outdated? Let us hold judgment on that. But for now, recall that Freud considered himself a healer of the "soul," the Greek Psyche, which has been Americanized into psychic conflict. Further, Murray Wax (1997), an anthropologist and psychoanalyst, has argued persuasively that the human mind has evolved slowly in the past few millennia.[7] We are still gripped by the human tales of Shakespeare's Hamlet or Lear, of King David's lust for Batsheva and his son Absalom's betrayal, of Abraham and Sarah's barren yearning for a child, and, of course, Oedipus's patricide and incestuous acts. Ancient tales resonate with something human inside us despite their antique origins. I will develop further that Maimonides's thoughts about the *structure* of the *Torah* and *how to reveal its secrets* carry similarities to Freud's ideas about dream structure and how to reveal truths that lie within.

The architecture of this book is as follows. I rely heavily on one of several papers by Leo Strauss, as well as Pines' English translation of the *Guide*. Strauss's 654-page volume of papers on Maimonides reveals his lifelong interest, even preoccupation with this thinker. Three Strauss papers, foundational to this chapter, developed more fully in Chapter 2, are entitled "The Literary Character of *The Guide of the Perplexed* (1941)"; "*Introduction to The Guide of the Perplexed* (1960)"; and "*How to Begin to Study the Guide of the Perplexed* (1963)".

Here, we will depend primarily on the "Literary Character" study. Like Alter's brilliant single-handed translation of the *Tanach* (*Torah, Nevi'im, and Ketuvim*), Strauss treats the *Guide* as a work of literature.[8] This permits Strauss to study semantics, syntax, characters, plot lines, and overall structure, like any great literary narrative.[9] He studies the architecture of the book's construction. This contrasts to religious studies of texts, which the orthodox treat as holy, the word of God, and hence incomparable.[10]

As Alter points out, as did Strauss, using a literary framework permits the student of the *Torah* or *Guide* to sidestep the arguments over the *Torah* was written by God, or by the hand of man guided by God (or even by the hand of man alone). Shifts in literary style and contradictions exist within the *Torah*. A fine writer (or adroit editors) can introduce stylistic changes, contradictions, even developmental shifts in greater knowledge as stylistic techniques that teach us something about the text. And in the humanistic studies, when we study a great text (*Torah* or *New Testament*, Virgil or Dante, Shakespeare), *we learn something about the human soul that resonates and enlarges our understanding of ourselves and humankind*. This is why Bloom referred to these texts as "wisdom literature" (Bloom, 2004). Aristotle pointed out that tragedy permits us vicarious emotional experiences. This is true for great literature.

On another vector, we benefit from Ricoeur's hermeneutic approach to Freud's writing: studying the text of the *Interpretation of Dreams* as if it were a text with embedded meanings that a hermeneutic approach can help unveil (Ricoeur, 1977; Szajnberg, 1996, 1997, 2010, 2018). By approaching both Freud's *Interpretation of Dreams* and Maimonides' *Guide* as literary texts, we can avail ourselves of hermeneutic comparisons. Yet, as we describe below, matters of the mind are not so simple—neither Freud's nor Maimonides'.

Begin with two fundamental commonalities between Maimonides' *Guide* and Freud's Irma dream in particular on representations in dreams.

First, Maimonides, like Freud, believes that oral dialogue is by far preferable to study either *Torah* or dreams (Strauss, 1963 p. 351).[11,12] Socrates' dialogue or Aristotle as the peripatetic philosopher would have been known to Maimonides. *This peripatia contrasts with the psychoanalytic technique but takes us beyond this book for the time being*. The written is a *forme fruste*, a degraded version of the oral dialogue and not as dynamic. Freud even asked that his patients should not write down their dreams. Strunk and White's *Elements of Style* (2005) would repeat this thrice to emphasize its importance: the oral/aural method gives us greater access to the poetic. In fact, the *Talmud*, while written, is written as a series of dialogues, even arguments. The *Torah* is read aloud thrice weekly and some study *Talmud* at double desks for debate.

Both texts—the *Guide* and the dream book—are *fundamentally about uncovering hidden "secrets."* Visual images are a specific technique of hiding matters in both *Guide/Torah* and dreams. The visual hides secrets *and* in order to understand the meaning behind the visual, one must articulate this into intelligible speech. Maimonides states at the beginning of his lengthy *Guide* that he will cover only two major passages: the Creation of the world and Ezekiel's (hallucinatory[13]) dream. Both passages are highly visual: like a dream reporter and analyzer, Maimonides concentrates on translating these into words and further into interpretations of the narratives. Dreams are ambiguous: they both conceal and reveal, just as Maimonides showed that *Torah* and his *Guide* both conceal and reveal. This is a cognitive/emotional shift (upward) from the more primitive visual to the developmentally advanced representation of words, speech, and stories. I will elaborate these two principles further, but fundamentally they underly the commonalities of these two texts or in fact three texts. Maimonides' *Guide* sees the *Torah* as also a text filled with secrets.

Here is another way to explicate the parallels between Maimonides' view of *Torah* and Freud's view of dreams. For Freud, remembered dreams are manifest. The latent lies beneath and can be discovered with specific techniques. And the latent is more meaningful than the manifest.[14] For Maimonides, the *Torah* is a manifest presentation (with laws that should be followed); hidden beneath is latent meaning, which can be explicated using the techniques described (but in a hidden format) by Maimonides. Yet, Erikson's (1954) profound contribution was that we can find hidden meaning even in the manifest "Irma" dream. And this explication can be accessed and used only by a select few who are highly trained. The latter description could have been applied to psychoanalytic training at one time and certainly is applicable to those who would know the *Torah* by heart, know Talmud, and also know Aristotle's reason and science.

For the moment, heuristically to stimulate our further investigation, let's consider this analogy: the *Torah is to dreams as the Guide is to Freud's dream book, specifically "Irma" but elaborated in Chapters* 5 through 6. Prior to Freud, many dream interpreters suggested that dream symbols show *how one should live one's life* (the dream as prophetic), Freud introduced the concept that dreams are visual manifestations of hidden interior wishes, thoughts, and feelings to be used to understand one's inner life. That is, Freud's idea about the visual[15] dream is that it "joins" the long history of esoteric "literature": narratives that have meanings that are hidden, yet also contain revealing information for the "educated" (Strauss, 1963; Halbertal, 2007; Lerner, 2000; Stern, 2018). Paradoxically, Freud pointed out that the dream is more determined by our ancient past (and day residue) and is "predictive" of our futures if uninterpreted or not understood. On the other hand, an understood (interpreted) dream "predicts" a future less encumbered by Unconscious wishes or impulses. So too Maimonides believed that the *Torah* had an explicit text about how to live one's life, what to "do," versus his *Guide's* view that the *Torah* had hidden meanings about how to think and believe. More specifically, to follow (without understanding) the *Torah* commandments and prohibitions is to follow out of fear of God. It is transactional: do good and you'll get good; do bad and you'll be punished. In contrast, to follow the subtleties of *Torah*—subtleties revealed through greater knowledge (including scientific knowledge)—is to follow *Torah* out of love and awe of God, as well as a more humble stance vis-à-vis the universe: man is decentered from the universe one that is not a *quid pro quo* transactional relationship with God (Halbertal, ibid.)

The analogy is not strictly accurate: Maimonides was renown for his earlier *Mishneh Torah*, which explicated the *Torah's* laws and how to do them. He goes further with the *Guide*, about how to think about the *Torah*. But both books—the *Guide* and the *Interpretation of Dreams*—are about interpretative techniques to uncover the hidden and more meaningful. A significant difference is that Maimonides revealed how to discover the hidden *Torah*; Freud allegedly revealed in writing how to discover the hidden (prohibited topics in Victorian Vienna), despite concern that he would be criticized or ostracized. I note "in writing" because I suggest that Freud revealed more of the fundamentals of interpretation embedded within the dialogue of transference in analyses.

One additional perhaps more subtle parallel among the texts (*Torah, Guide*, Dream book) is that while much takes place in dreams (and *Torah*) with visual images, it is predominately, perhaps *only* via articulated words between humans that the underlying meanings are transmitted and hence understood. That is, a fundamental "translation" must happen from image to word (and further to understanding the concept and feeling beneath the word) so that a full understanding of the Biblical story/dream can take place. In practice, the *Torah* is read aloud in a community. And, as Walter Benjamin remarked, *traduttore, traditore*, translation is a traitor. How often do we hear from analysands (or ourselves) that the dream report lacks something from the dream remembered and experienced?

Here's a further parallel between Maimonides' attitude toward the Biblical text and Freud's toward the "psychoanalytic text," whether dream or parapraxis. Psychoanalysts are a suspicious—or at least inquisitive—species: any dream, slip, or remark means both itself and something (more meaningful often) that is not stated, or stated in disguise. Maimonides turns our view of the Bible around or at least makes it more complex: each Biblical remark certainly means what it says ("Thou shalt not kill"), yet *also speaks in parables, enigmas.* Maimonides tries to teach us that to fully understand the *Torah* means to decode its parabolic and enigmatic layers. Both Freud and Maimonides are on a trail of the unspoken, the hidden, the disguised, to reach *the more meaningful.* Before turning to specific techniques of concealment in the *Torah/Guide* that anticipate Freud's comments on dream work (and subsequent interpretation to "undo" the work), let us look at Maimonides' account of why he wrote this *Guide.*

To be clear, I suggest here that there may be something inherent in the more hallucinatory or imaginative visual dream images we create that in order to understand them, we must narrate these into word stories. This was an insight for both Maimonides and Freud.

Maimonides was previously renown for writing the *Mishneh Torah,*[16] his detailed account of all 613 laws[17] in the *Torah* and how to follow on both prohibitions and commandments, the negatives and positives. How does the *Guide* differ? The *Mishneh Torah* is *Halacha,* the "science of the law" (p. 344), of praxis. The *Guide* is *agada,* the *true* science of the law, which *tells the reasons* beneath commands and prohibitions. The Hebrew root of *Halacha* is *holech,* to walk, or how to walk the path of life in a "lawful" manner (Strauss, 1963, p. 344).[18] There is hidden wisdom in the root of *Halacha* akin to Aristotle's peripatesis.

The Hebrew root of *agada* is *l'hagid,* to tell, as in "to tell a story." And stories are to be spoken, for Maimonides, the preferable way to teach. The premise of the *Guide* is to reconcile *praxis,* the actions of the law, with reason, which for Maimonides meant Aristotle. *Torah* is about what to *do;* the *Guide* is about what *to think and believe* (Maimonides 2.10; II a-b, 3-5; Strauss, p. 344).[19,20] Of the many secrets of *Torah,* the two major secrets the entire *Guide* tackles (both concealing and revealing) are the *ma'aseh bereshit* (the matter (or "doing") of Creation) and the *ma'aseh merkavah* (the matter (or "doing") of the chariot). The Chariot story alludes to Ezekiel's vision of ascending to heaven on a fiery chariot and seeing the Lord seated on a throne. Alter refers to the latter as the most hallucinatory in the *Tanach.* Let us accept that for Maimonides, Creation was the greatest of miracles (and if one includes the Adam and Eve story, prophetic of mankind); the Ezekiel story, one of the most remarkable of prophetic visions, topping Isaiah's. For Maimonides, these two visions are equivalent to Freud's Irma dream: remarkable visual narratives which can be translated into narratives, thereby revealing what's hidden within. Freud turned to other dreams in the dream book, but he devoted an entire chapter to the Irma dream and kept returning to it. In *Torah,* look at how *visual* is the story of Creation (*tohu v'vohu* (emptiness and void)); the sky, the seas separated from the earth; flying or other animals, the serpent first on legs, then condemned to belly-crawl; the nakedness of Adam and Eve—its visual (genital revelation leading to their exile). After all, the specific "knowledge"

Adam and Eve gain from their oral transgression is that they *see* their nakedness. It is a visual transgression to begin. These are parallel to Freud's dream images.

Further, these two stories, per Maimonides, cover two fundamental disciplines: physics (the Creation of the world, including the laws of physics that govern us) and metaphysics (the Chariot story that brings us closer to understanding God and his angels).

Here, we will offer only a gloss on the *Guide* to demonstrate some parallels to the Dream book. We develop this in Chapter 2 on the *Guide*. To give an understanding of the *Guide*, as Strauss confesses, would take a book-length study. (But a psychoanalyst might say the same about understanding the inner life of humankind.)

Freud offers early in his dream book how the dream work proceeds: with predominately visual, hidden symbols, and metaphors, even parables that both conceal and reveal (Freud, 1900). *For Freud, visual thoughts are made conscious through words/language.* Well, let us then begin with examples from Maimonides of how the *Bible* and his *Guide* engage in the same kind of "visually revelatory" "work" of concealment.

First, a breathtaking statement by Maimonides that matches Freud's dictum that dreams are mostly visual (and hence a way of hiding words or more so thoughts, feelings, and particularly wishes). A complementary idea from Freud is that thoughts are made conscious through words/language. Dan Stern (1985), describing the development of four levels of self, articulated the paradoxic that at the fourth level, upon achieving fuller speech, there is a *distancing* from earlier levels of self. Maimonides states that *all Torah visual descriptions* of God, particularly anything alluding to human characteristics, are misleading and are *not true.* He challenges popular (mis)understandings of the *Torah* further, stating that *God can only be understood by what he is not.* Most *Torah* readers might respond (in surprise) that the *Torah* states that God created man in his image; that God is described visually as sitting upon a throne, and Moses was shown the back of God; for Ezekiel, God sits on his throne.

Misleading balderdash, Maimonides insists. He argues that God is like no other being on earth nor in the universe: any human description of him is but a symbol or metaphor to facilitate humankind's understanding of God. *And, these visual images also mislead our understanding.* This paradox haunts the *Torah* reader through the *Guide*.

We come to another paradoxical premise of the *Guide*. Maimonides states that he will explore the reasons behind the commandments and prohibitions. Yet, one of the prohibitions in the *Torah* is that an entire set of laws, *Chukim*, should not be explained! How does Maimonides, an observant Jew, address this prohibition? He sidesteps it by not calling the *Guide* a book, but rather in Judeo-Arabic a *maquala* (*ma'amar* in proper Hebrew). *Ma'amar* is from the Hebrew root, *amar*, to say, or a speech. Both *agada* and *ma'amar* put Maimonides' *Guide* in the realm of the spoken. And for Maimonides, hints are more easily embedded in oral teaching and more valuable than the explicit statement of written texts. The *Guide* is Maimonides' "attempt to revive the oral discussion" (Strauss, 1963 p. 353). This reminds us that psychoanalysis as an oral discussion of the patient's unconscious (which we can think of as an esoteric text/narrative) manifests through dreams, fantasies, transference, and other components.[21]

Maimonides' major premise is that the *Torah* is wrought with hidden secrets; the *Guide* will aid the educated student to uncover the secrets embedded within the text. Therefore, a major component of the *Guide* is to describe how secrets are hidden. I ask the psychoanalytic reader to listen with an inner ear (or Reik's Third Ear (Reik, 1983)) to hear parallels to Freud's account of dream work—the mechanisms by which the Ego hides Unconscious, unacceptable, secret wishes. We find a remarkable resonance with this prescient, medieval text.

One technique used in *Torah/Tanach* to hide matters is *repetition or rather variations on a theme*. For instance, in the "Job" story, four "friends" visit him at the same time and try to convince him to renounce God after Job's entire family and livestock have been wiped out. But Eliphaz, Bildad, Zophar, and Elihu only appear to give the same reasons. When Maimonides asks us to read more carefully, we find that there are variations among the arguments of the four friends.[22] And the variations—here Maimonides is a prescient Freud—tell us that it is *within the slippage of the apparently minor differences that we will find the true message* of the story. Another Maimonides example is the repetition of the Creation story, but with variations. And a further example is how Ezekiel repeats his hallucinatory celestial vision, but with slight variation. And Ezekiel's vision is a variation of Isaiah's earlier vision. Rather than see this as "errors" in the Bible's account, like the analyst, Maimonides seeks meaning in the variations, even "slips" of repetition. We might call these textual parapraxes.

This reminds us of Freud's (1900) suggestion that when a dream seems unclear to us, we ask the dreamer to repeat it: when we hear variations, we can suspect that the Ego hints at significant material at those shears of the dream's layers. Asking the analysand to repeat the dream will reveal slight slippages and variations, along which we will discover fuller meaning. Explore the shears to get more readily at what is being concealed/revealed by the Ego.

Maimonides sees the *Torah* (and writes his *Guide*) as "repeating conventional statements ... *to hide the disclosure* ... of unconventional views" (Strauss, 1964, p. 367, author's italics). So too, we can say, Freud discovered in the mundane (parapraxes, dreams) ways of hiding the disclosure of unconventional views. Further, Maimonides believes that "to grasp the totality ... (one must) grasp each word which occurs ..." (368–369). Again, these are techniques familiar to good psychoanalytic work.

Maimonides offers three other techniques of Biblical obfuscation of hidden meaning: *secrets, contradictions, and irregularities.* Here we summarize what we will expand in the next few Maimonides chapters.

Let us start with the simpler obfuscation, irregularities. In a long series of chapters on God's place and types of movement, the *Guide* interrupts with a section on the meaning of "man." In *Judges*, mourning laws are inserted. These irregularities happen in *Torah*, for instance in the over 40 chapters of the "Joseph" story. Suddenly, after Joseph is sold into slavery by his brothers (they reconsidering their plan to murder him), there is an entire chapter on Judah's virtual incest with Tamar after she deceives him (Szajnberg, 2018). Without entering the details of Maimonides' exploration of the meaning of these interruptions, let us say that, like Freud, he finds meaning hidden (and also betraying what is hidden) to reveal "a deeper order, meaning" (Strauss, 2013, p. 363). Alter, an astute scholar of the *Torah*, is puzzled by the Judah/Tamar chapter. In a recent book on Jacob and Joseph, I (Szajnberg, 2018) suggested that this intrusive tale tells us what happens when that overseer, Joseph, is removed from the family. Yet, it also tells us the power of this near-incest: Judah, the father-in-law, impregnates Tamar, whose two husbands (Judah's sons) died shortly after her wedding them (specifically after intercourse) and generations later, the fruit of her womb is King David.[23] This nuanced tale hints at both the transgressive act and its fortunate (redemptive?) outcome. This Judah/Tamar interlude puzzled Alter (2019), an astute literary scholar. But it (Szajnberg, ibid.) offers an explanation from a psychoanalytic perspective. With this, let's return to Maimonides and Freud.

Pause to look at how Maimonides understood the literary structure of the *Torah* before we can explore the hiding methods further.

For Maimonides, the *Torah* is mostly written as parables and enigmas. In fact, Strauss uses the term "parabolic" to describe Maimonides' view of *Torah* structure. And a parabola is an indirect way to connect two points. While it is not as simple as a line, it has geometric laws governing its path ($y = x$ squared), as do the parables or enigmas of the *Torah*. It is the "formula" for the parables or enigmas of the *Torah* that guides the *Guide*. So too Maimonides explored the geometry, the logic, that uncover the laws that govern the writing of the *Torah*.

Now the method of the *Guide*. Maimonides deliberately chooses *not* to write it in parables or enigmas, as this would simply copy the *Torah's* structure. Rather, he chose to write with obscurity and brevity. So he says, but then proceeds to use parables (Halbertal, 2019). Also, *contradictions* can be a substitute for parables. And Maimonides' contradictions are elaborate and complex (Strauss, 1960). Finally, Maimonides insists that parsimony will more likely lead to the truth.

Here is an obvious *contradiction*. Maimonides states that the *Guide* covers two subjects and two subjects only: *ma'aseh bereshit* and *ma'aseh merkava*, the story of Creation and the story of the chariot (Ezekiel's visions), both are highly visual, even hallucinatory events "translated" or transformed into words. He further states that studying *ma'aseh bereshit* is like studying physics; studying *ma'aseh merkava* is studying metaphysics (by which he means Divine knowledge (of God and the angels)). *Then*, he states that the *Guide will not* be about physics nor metaphysics! Strauss offers some guidance. When there are contradictions, the answer must be one or the other (not some compromise in between). And since we know from reading the *Guide* that it is almost entirely about what Maimonides considered the two greatest miracles or prophetic visions—the Creation of the universe and Ezekiel's dream/hallucination—we know that Maimonides is writing about them and hence about physics and metaphysics. But why write this contradiction? As mentioned, Maimonides wrote in an era when writing about certain aspects of the *Torah* to explain it (including God's incorporeal being) would result in his being excommunicated (a *kherem* placed on him). His contradictions offer deniability and some protection (Meltzer, 2014).[24] This may be similar to Freud's efforts in his work with hysteria at a time when hysteria was almost an anathema topic and certainly thought to be a physical ailment, popularized by one of Freud's teachers, Charcot.

Strauss identifies at least *six ways* in which Maimonides *conceals via contradictions*. We ask the reader to bear with brief descriptions of the *mechanisms* used by Maimonides to hide contradictions (and simultaneously leave crumbs for us to follow the paths to revealing secrets). As we list these six techniques, let us keep in mind how much they resonate with Freud's account of how in dreams (and parapraxes) significant meanings are both hidden and revealed.

First, one can speak of the same subject in a contradictory manner, but on pages far from each other. Second, a variation: make "one of the two contradictory statements in passing" (Strauss, 1964, p. 373). (Here, consider Freud's focus on the "passing" remark in his Irma dream "at once" and focus on this brief phrase.) Third, contradict an initial statement by contradicting its implications (by indirection). Fourth, contradicting by repeating the statement, but with a meaningful omission or addition.[25] Fifth, a variation on the fourth, is to place an intermediary remark between two contradictory statements, such that the intermediate statement points the reader toward Maimonides' true meaning. Sixth, to conceal via contradictions, Maimonides used ambiguous words (and the category of ambiguous words is expanded later by Maimonides. Of course, the nature of ambiguity (words or statements) is one of Freud's major clinical discoveries from the Dream book onwards. We give but one example here of how to figure out which of the two statements is true. Maimonides states that a fundamental basis for all contradictions in the *Guide* (and hence a hint to decoding these) is the contradiction between *true teaching based on reason* versus *untrue teaching based on imagination*. And, true teachings are secret and are rare.

Therefore, if we read two apparently contradictory statements in the *Guide*, we can ferret out that the *statement that is less frequent or even stated once is the secret and hence true statement*. Maimonides gives two examples of this from *Tanach*.

1   The belief in the resurrection of the dead (Maimonides believes this is true at the end of times) is stated only *once* in *Tanach*, in two verses of Daniel.
2   The statement "The Lord is one," upon which Jews believe in God's unity, is *not* repeated in the *Torah*.

Let us turn to one other (of many) techniques that Maimonides identifies in the *Torah* and uses in his *Guide* to disguise and reveal truths, the use of hints. Maimonides gives four examples of *hints* used in words alone (there are more techniques used in sentences or paragraphs).

1   Secret words used in ambiguous ways. For instance, a single word can pivot us from one category of thought to another. *Al-af-al*—meaning actions from the commandments—is a pivotal term that shifts our attention from sections on *opinions* to sections on *actions*. Or, the ambiguous Arabo-Judaic term "*amr*" can mean either a thing or a command. (This is similar to the Hebrew *davar*, which may mean "word" or "thing." It is famously used in the Jacob Joseph story after Joseph's second dream of having the moon, sun, and eleven stars bow to him. He is first reprimanded by Jacob, then we are told that Jacob kept this *davar* (word, thing) in mind.) But we recall that Freud believed that "words" bring "things" into consciousness.
2   *Apostrophes* or *mottoes*: these are used in the original Greek sense. An apostrophe is an exclamatory address to a dead or absent subject, as well as a turning away, an elision; mottoes are prefixed to words and these short phrases in order to encapsulate a belief or ideal.
3   Silence or omission. For instance, Maimonides partially quotes Aristotle to mislead the uninformed reader to think that Maimonides agrees with Aristotle's belief that (sexual) touch is a bad thing. But the scholar (of Aristotle) would know that a full quote reveals that Maimonides believes the opposite, disagrees with Aristotle, based on Jewish beliefs.
4   Chapter headings that allude to or misdirect the casual reader. Maimonides' historical situation explains his technique. Rabbis insisted that the secrets of the *Torah* can only be alluded to by chapter headings (not full explication). Maimonides minuets around this, risking excommunication. He gives chapter headings pregnant with meaning; writes allusive chapters.

Now, to Freud's Irma dream to see one parallel between both Freud's explication of how "distorting" dream work happens *and* how Freud's interpretative technique untangles the hidden meaning. We will cover Freud in more detail later, but offer here a sample of the resonance of his text with Maimonides on mental mechanisms. We will see a parallel between Maimonides technique of critical reading of the *Torah* and his technique of hiding/revealing in the *Guide*.

The Irma dream covers two-thirds of a page, followed by *ten* pages of interpretation and a final discovery, not just of the latent (hidden) meaning of this dream, but also the motive and structure of all dreams as wishes and motives. From the phrase, "I at once called on Dr. M....", Freud extracts two words "at once." A naive reader (as we are without *his* associations) might pass over these relatively neutral two words. Instead, Freud's point is:

"...'at once' was sufficiently striking to require a special exploration."

Then, he associates to "a tragic event in my practice...about the death of a patient..." (with the same name as his eldest daughter, who died several years later).

"At once," we might say, has a tenor similar to the *Torah*'s **Hineini,** here I am. "Here I am" seems a straightforward phrase to the naive reader. But, to those who know its use in *Torah*, we recall that whenever a character says this one word—which Alter (2019) calls a "pointing word"—a momentous, even almost tragic event will occur: Abraham almost sacrifices Isaac, Joseph agrees to his father's request to oversee his brothers' work and is sold into slavery and thought dead by his father, and so on.

Again, we pivot from *Torah* to Freud's observations on dreams (or hysteria): disguise permits recognition.

Another *Torah* phrase that seems straightforward but to the knowledgable reader takes on premonitory meaning is *"yifet to'ar v'yifet mar'eh,"*[26] "appeared handsome/beautiful in appearance." This seems straightforward; then we notice a narrative pattern. When Rachel is called *"yifet to'ar v'yifet mar'eh,"* she suffers years of infertility, begging her husband, Jacob, for a child (and rebuked by him). Decades later, when Rachel's favored son, Joseph, is described similarly, he is a slave in Egypt, just prior to being accused wrongly by his master's wife of attempting rape. The knowledgable reader knows these terms or phrases have manifest meanings in themselves, but have deeper, latent, and more ominous meanings. Not so good, perhaps, to be good-looking in the *Torah*. Or, not so good, but things work out for the Jewish people: Rachel dies in childbirth, but her son goes on to lead his people; Joseph is jailed for seven years after the wrongful allegation, but then emerges as a Viceroy in Egypt and saves his Jewish people. Maybe bad for the character, but good for the Jewish people is a hidden *Torah* message.[27]

While we may not find one-to-one correspondences between the terms for hidden or manifest/latent that Maimonides and Freud use, our intent is to see that the *techniques and concepts are similar*. Freud concentrates on two words—"at once"— that have manifest meanings but contain a latent and deeper meaning. *Torah* looks at one word, or phrase, that has manifest reasonable meaning, but has latent, more significant meaning. These Freud examples would fit the Maimonides category of planting hints within words. For instance, look at *"hineini!"* This exclamatory is superficially addressed from Joseph to Jacob, but may also be considered addressed to the "absent" figure of God, an example of what Strauss calls *apostrophe*. *Hineini* also encapsulates a belief system (an example of Strauss's *mottoes*): one is "here" not only physically, but also "here" in full faith, unquestioningly ... even if it emerges that one has volunteered (unwittingly?) to sacrifice one's son. In the Irma dream, the entire dream is filled with words and phrases that are manifestly addressed to the dreamer *and* latently *addressed to the dreamer who was "absent" during the dream but must be very present when awake in order to interpret it.*

Let's look at contradictions as a biblical technique, per Maimonides, and Freud's use of contradiction in the Irma dream. Freud *sees* a character who appears "pale and puffy" in the dream. He *recalls* that this Irma character does not look that way in waking life and thus concludes "it must be someone else." That is, within the dream, there is a *contradiction between the visual and the remembered name.* The "white patch on the turbinates" (of Irma) in fact belongs to someone else and furthers his "secret": he'd prefer to replace Irma with another person. Again we have a "contradiction" between the visual and the named person.

Further examples follow Maimonides' exposition of hiding, using words, particularly omissions or (misleading) chapter headings. In "Irma," Freud notes an odd word replacement, "pain." On analysis, this word is a screen for "nausea, disgust," in the real Irma. And even in his recurrent use of "Irma," he notes an attempt to "mislead" his awakened, dream-remembering self from the *wish to substitute a number of other* (more compliant) patients for Irma. Interestingly, even Freud's footnote that one may reach the "navel" of a dream, where it becomes unknowable, reminds us of Maimonides' recurrent warning, even emphasis, that at least to most Jewish believers, the fundamental secrets of the *Torah* may be unknowable ... possibly even to the most knowledgable believers. But analysts strive to uncover hidden meanings in order to live fuller lives.

We can amend Freud's conclusion at the end of Chapter 5, "Dreams really have a meaning." What he has demonstrated is that dreams have two meanings ... the manifest meaning and more significantly, the latent meaning.[28] In parallel, we can conclude that about Maimonides, for he wrote two major books on *Torah*: the *Mishne Torah*, about manifest meanings; the *Guide*, about latent meanings. This is similar to Freud's approach to revealing Unconscious meaning.

Here, psychoanalytic readers might pause and remind us that much that we have written about concealment or censorship in Maimonides is quite familiar to the student of Freud. As early as 1895, Freud used the term "censorship" (albeit interchangeably with "defense") as a characteristic of dreams (and later he expands this to symptomatic acts). By 1900, Freud states that dreams are composed with dissimulation; coded messages help evade the *internal* censor. He turns to his beloved Goethe, when Freud confesses, "When I interpret my dreams for my readers, I am obliged to adopt similar distortions." [Goethe] complains of the need for these distortions in the words: "After all the best of what you know may not be told to boys."

Freud then turns from internal censorship to external:

> "...the political writer who has disagreeable truths to tell ... must beware of censorship ... must soften the expression of his opinion. According to the strength and sensitivity of the censorship, he finds himself compelled either to refrain from certain framers of attack, or to speak in allusions ... or must conceal his objectionable pronouncement beneath some apparently innocent disguise.... *The stricter the censorship, the more far reaching will be the disguise and the more ingenious too may be the means employed for **putting the reader on the scent of the true** **meaning**."*

I add italics to emphasize the *censor's* reaction to the author's intention and then bold-faced the author's attempt to help the *reader* decode the censored meaning. There is tension. The tension between the author's honest intent, the censor's work, versus the (honest) reader's and author's "'collusion" to evade the censorship (Strauss, 1952). Just as there is tension between the Ego's work to hide and its work to reveal. This is true for Freud (speaking of dream work, but also of his need to speak the impolite, the socially unacceptable to the reader). And this is so true for the medieval Maimonides, who also was trying to evade the censorships of critical rabbis,[29] and earlier in his life, of Moorish Moslems who forced the conversion of Jews in Spain from which his family fled. Even after being safely in Egypt, Maimonides addressed the same life-death issues of conversion under threat of death among the Yemenite Jews facing the invading Moslems *(Iggeret Temani, 1189)*. There are intriguing parallels between Maimonides the man and his work with Freud's crises and creativity.

Discussion

We describe four prescient descriptions of "mental" mechanisms for hiding/revealing by Maimonides of *Torah* text—prescient of Freud's account of dream work, focusing on the Irma dream. These are as follows:

1 An emotionally important text (*Torah* or dream) has both latent and manifest (hidden) meanings.
2 Oral recounting of the texts is the best method to uncover hidden meanings, although both Maimonides and Freud "settle" for written recounting.

3 There is a logical set of mechanisms to hide manifest texts and this hiding contains within it revealing hints *for those well-trained in the texts.*

4 What is hidden is unacceptable to the reader/dreamer *and even to society, which would reject, even excommunicate, the revealer.*

Yet, those who seek greater knowledge (of *Torah*, or inner life) must confront the resistance in order to lead more meaningful, informed lives.

We offered parallels between Maimonides' description of (mental) mechanisms for how to hide meanings within the text (e.g., ambiguous terms; omissions; contradictions; misleading chapter headings) and Freud's description of dream works' Unconscious (and possibly even conscious) mechanisms to hide meanings. We can remind ourselves that when Freud describes hiding mechanisms, he also articulates revealing techniques that ferret out the deeper latent meanings. That is, per Freud and Maimonides, if we know the mechanisms of hiding, we can also discover the revealing hints within what is hidden, provided we are trained (and courageous enough to face the deeper meanings). Maimonides uses terms such as metaphor, parable, and enigma to describe hiding mechanisms in the *Torah* text. These could be applied to dream secrets and their unraveling.

We suggest several conclusions in this chapter which will be developed in the following chapters. Some appear heterodox.

First, we can think of the *Torah* as great literature (written by a man or by God for man). Hence, it is a Creation of a mind (Auerbach, 1954), a measure of internal life at a certain time, of a certain culture. The text is a measure of era and beliefs. Then we would expect that it would contain within its structure complex layers from manifest through latent, with sophisticated, even engaging techniques of being able to be read interestingly at multiple levels by multiple audiences (Bloom, 2004). Homer's *Iliad* can be read as a gory tale, an ethical righting of woman theft, Odysseus' Trojan cleverness, or at other levels depending on the audience. It endures.

Second, Maimonides, as a literary critic, figured out the multiple layers of meaning in *Torah*. As Strauss suggests in his writing on totalitarianism, Maimonides hid his findings to avoid excommunication.[30,31] Freud wrote what he discovered and experienced disapprobation.

Third, Maimonides' account of mechanisms of hiding secrets within a text is stunningly similar to Freud's account of Unconscious mechanisms with dreams. We may explain this both by Maimonides' genius and his addressing the most meaningful text to him as a Jew, the *Torah*. In this sense, Freud's most meaningful text (beginning in his forties and throughout his life) was his inner life, including as it was illuminated by his dreams.

Fourth, Freud, who overtly abjured his Jewish education (Richards, 2022), we now know, was well-educated in the *Torah* at least, even using the book inscribed to him by his father. Is it possible that Freud was acquainted with the levels of meaning in the *Torah*, possibly even the techniques the writer(s) used to hide/reveal meanings in the *Torah*? We do not know if Freud read Maimonides,[32] he did not have to if he had been as careful a reader of *Torah* as he was of other texts.[33] Freud confessed that much of what he discovered about the mind was found in fiction, particularly the nineteenth-century literature. But he also said that when faced with a particularly opaque or apparently meaningless dream, he treated this as if it were a holy text (Bakan, 1975). Further historical research can clarify if he also learned from his study of the *Torah*.

We do not argue for continuity of esoterica tradition from Maimonides *influencing* Freud. Rather, there are interesting analogies, not strict linearly per Gilman (2020). If we conceptualize both Maimonides and Freud studying "texts" that illuminate the inner lives of man (the *Torah, Guide,* dream), then there will be nodes of analogy that thoughtful scholars will come upon at different human eras. Gilman, a historian, continues, "history consists of radical ruptures and hidden as well as open continuities; ... many by-ways as highways" (Gilman, 2020).

Another level with which to understand Maimonides' thinking is by considering his study of one of his most important life texts, the *Torah, as a reflection of his inner life, as a path to understand this man.* This resembles Didier-Anzieu's (1986) deeply insightful study of Freud, Freud's self-analysis, and birthing psychoanalysis. Didier-Anzieu reveals "... that the central passage ... on screen memories, *Über Deckerinnerungen* (1899a), was ... disguised autobiographical account." That is, Dider-Anzieu's overall research approach to learning about Freud and psychoanalysis was to examine Freud's texts as a reflection of what was most important to the man. This is a speculative step for us in the discussion: if we study Maimonides' ideas and passion about his most beloved text, the *Torah,* we can learn something about this man's inner life. It is another path to the most intimate autobiography. We are aided by Halbertal's scholarly study of Maimonides—first biographical fragments, then all of Maimonides' studies. To our good fortune, letters and manuscripts in Maimonides' own hand, with written redactions, were discovered in the Cairo *geniza*.[34] *Maimonides'* letters, particularly to his beloved student Joseph for whom he wrote the *Guide*, reveal a man with humor, as well as the man mourning his brother's death for over a year, and not fully recovering. The latter I will touch on to draw a parallel to Freud.

In our next chapter, we turn in detail to Maimonides' life: how did his life influence his work? How did Maimonides transform life's vicissitudes into creative acts as did Freud?

Prior to the pivotal crisis in Maimonides' life, his brother's tragic death (and family's loss of income), when Maimonides was 39, I offer a sweeping summary of his life's vicissitudes and how this contributed to his thinking.

Maimonides was born in Andalusia and descended from an illustrious intellectual line. When the Moors invaded, importing a severe Islam with forced conversion of Jews, Maimonides escaped to the Maghreb.[35] His life continued as an immigrant refugee as he moved to Egypt, briefly to Israel, and returned to Egypt. In Egypt, despite being "foreign" to the Jewish community, he earned such respect that eventually he was appointed head of the community on two occasions and others turned to him for Jewish religious decisions.

One such decision helps us understand how his life vicissitudes affected his opinions of the Jewish community. Some rabbis ruled that Jews faced with conversion under life that should select death instead.[36] Maimonides objected. Influenced by his own and his family's experiences, he insisted that a Jew who converts under life threat should not be considered a "convert." Rather he remained a Jew. He cited *Tanach* to support his opinion: "I have set before you life and death, blessings and curses. *Now choose life,* so that you and your children may live" (Deut. 30:19). (Alter, 2019).

But let us turn to Maimonides' most severe trauma, the death of his brother, to see how this parallels Freud's loss of his daughter Sophie (and decades prior, his father's death) and how both turned such grief into one of their more creative endeavors.

Maimonides' brother, David, supported the extended family, releasing Maimonides to write. In 1177, when Maimonides was 39, David drowned in the Indian Ocean. After a year of almost prostrate with mourning, Maimonides returned to practice as a physician, eventually to Egyptian royalty (Halbertal, 2014). More remarkably, he turned to writing *The Guide*, the second pinnacle of his life's work, after the *Mishneh Torah*. He wrote the *Guide* despite his need to work extraordinary hours as a physician and his continued (unpaid) work as a Rabbi and head of the Jewish community.[37] We can speculate that Maimonides transformed his profound mourning into the creativity of the *Guide*. We recall that Freud wrote his *Interpretation* after his father's death; perhaps more profoundly after the sudden death of his beloved daughter, Sophie, in 1920, Freud initiated the significant transformation of his ideas of the psyche's structure that culminated in *The Ego and the Id* (1923). Just as Maimonides' *Guide* was a significant intellectual shift from his own *Mishne Torah*, so Freud's *Ego and Id* was a significant shift from his earlier works that resulted in a revised theory of mind.

Following Didier-Anzieu, this shift reflected a change in Freud's inner life after his understanding of mourning (Freud, 1917) after the losses of World War I; more so, after Sophie's death.

We offer a more modest conclusion: that Maimonides' account of narrative mechanisms of hiding and revealing in the *Torah* was remarkably similar to Freud's account of dream mechanisms, particularly the Irma dream. At first approximation, we could say that Maimonides discovered these hiding/revealing techniques consciously, while Freud described (predominately) Unconscious techniques in dream work. Yet, from what we have learned about creative thinking/writing like Maimonides', the Unconscious/

Preconscious contributes to creativity (Kris, 1950; Giovacchini, 1971). Freud remarked, "... the inside of the ego which comprises above all the intellectual processes has the quality of being preconscious" (Freud, 1939, p. 42).

Intriguingly, a corollary is that Freud in his dream discoveries, particularly the "esoteric," concealing/revealing quality of dreams, may have picked up a quality of imaginative narrative described from Plato onward: that a *daemon* invades or inhabits the narrator to create the new ideas/stories. (I emphasize "narrator," following Plato on Homer's sung *Odyssey*, the peripatetic Aristotle, Maimonides, even the cantorial reciters of *Torah* today: audiences respond to something unique about song transmission. While writing down these narratives may memorialize them, they may also *diminish* the liveliness.) Freud may be in a long line of those who discover in creative, challenging narratives the need to conceal and the ability to reveal.

Maimonides, this twelfth-century literary genius, may have discovered from his study of *Torah* what Freud discovered in his study of dreams.[38] The first two of Maimonides' 13 principles for Judaism are: God is one and incorporeal. Applied to ourselves: *we* are one, not multiple selves; *our* souls/psyche feel immaterial, but compelling. This is a "translation" of Maimonides' concepts from "polytheism" to monotheism, or in our terms, from multiple impulses/selves to one self who struggles with impulses. Further study of Maimonides may reveal to what degree he could use the *Torah* as a proxy of his inner life, which he learned to "read" as Freud did his own inner life through his dream "texts." We will discuss these greater realizations about our inner life as a unity (with tensions and divisions), yet embodied in the corporeal, even as we may strive for some "incorporeal" sense of our selves, a living together of body and soul, that Freud discovered we can achieve.

What do we know of this man Maimonides that may shed light on his significant works? Let's turn to his life.

Notes

1   Dream research has progressed subsequent to Freud's work, as summarized by Blechner (2013): "Psychoanalysis has greatly revised its theory of dream formation and the clinical approach to working with dreams, including the role of disguise in dream formation and the need for associations in dream understanding. Both the Freudian and the activation-synthesis models of dream formation are two-stage; neither two-stage model may best account for the data." For this chapter, we focus on Freud's early ideas about dream work. Nevertheless, as Stimmel (1996, p.77) summarizes, "The central challenge of dream analysis is how to bridge the gap between these very different modes of thought ... and impose *waking meaning* on *sleeping thought*." We differ with the idea of "impose" waking meaning on sleeping thought. The proper interpretation should fit with the sleeping thought, not feel imposed upon, as we attempt to do in this book comparing Maimonides and Freud.

2   Freud pulled back from this position, but reinstated it in later works (Auchinclass and Samberg, p. 64).

3 Yet, Freud believed that true mastery of dream interpretation took place in the dialogue of the clinical setting, more so than in a written text on technique. Maimonides states strongly in the introduction to his *Guide that the proper way to transmit such knowledge is by dialogue.* His written text is a compromise, pressed by the diaspora and the persecution of Jews within both the Islamic Maghreb and also Christian states. Freud never wrote a book about 'technique" perhaps because he knew that like any discipline—physics, music, dance—mastery must be learned in practice with masters, not reading a text.

4 So too Freud felt "excommunicated" by both colleagues and members of polite Viennese society after his outrageous statements about our inner lives and wishes. Some analytic historians dispute the degree of Freud's isolation. (Gay,1998; Makari, 2008, 2013). We recall that even in the (early) Enlightenment, Galileo tried to hide his discoveries from the Church by writing in mirror handwriting, a technique not sufficient to keep the Church from condemning him to home quarantine. Much earlier, Jesus stated that he spoke in parables for the public, but spoke the "truth" to his disciples. "I speak to them (the hoi palloi) in parables, because seeing they do not see, and hearing, they do not hear, nor do they understand" (Matt. 13:10-12). Earlier these words were "borrowed" and transformed from Psalms 135:16, Isaiah 6; 10-10; Proverbs 23:9) as is often the case in New Testament (unattributed) quotes. As analysts, we are not surprised that the oppressed (Jesus and his disciples) would over time become the oppressor. (The Church and Galileo, the Church's immolation of Giordano Bruno among others. Jew murderers, including the Romans who murdered the Jewish Christ, then over a million other Jewish citizens, demonstrated the danger of revealing overtly one's beliefs.)

5 That is, even for his treasured disciple, Yossef, Maimonides not only disguised the *Guide* from the common man, but *even* from his own disciple. Yossef would have to study avidly to understand all or most of what Maimonides hid and hinted. Further, Maimonides argued that the *Torah* was written in this manner. And in *New Testament*, Jesus says overtly to his own 12 disciples, "I have yet many things to say to you, but *you cannot bear them now*" (John 16:12).

6 There is active debate in the history of knowledge between those who seek linearity or continuities in ideas versus considering history as one of "... radical ruptures and hidden as well as open continuities; there are as many byways as highways (Makari, 2015; Gilman, personal communication 2020). We assume the latter, more modest stance. Fishbane (2003) suggests the concept that "topological comparisons may underscore similarities …. without the need to assert or presume hidden influences in the absence of evidence" (pp. 207–208).

7 Yuval Harrari's *Sapiens* (2014) suggests that over millennia, there are some shifts in human behavior and thinking such as from hunter/gatherer to agricultural existence.

8 Strauss expressed gratitude to Emil Fackenheim and his colleague (of his refugee Chicago years) Allan Bloom.

9 Borges in *This Craft of Verse* (2002) also treated *Torah* with the same respect as he did other great literary works, permitting cross-comparisons.

10 However, the religious will compare their own holy text to others, generally in unfavorable ways. For instance, a religious Christian will read the *Torah* as a *forme fruste* of the New Testament; the *Torah* predicts the truth of the New Testament (Auerbach, 2013).

11 That Socrates engaged in dialogue and Aristotle was known as the peripatetic philosopher would have been known to Maimonides. This peripatia contrasts with psychoanalytic technique, but takes us beyond this chapter for the time being.

12 "The inferiority of writing is also indicated by the designation of those biblical works which had not been composed by prophets proper as 'writings'" (Strauss, 1963, 351).

13 "Hallucinatory" is Alter's (2019) term for Ezekiel's highly visual account of his traveling to heaven and seeing God enthroned.

14 Erikson's (1954) profound contribution was that we can find hidden meaning even in the manifest dream; his paper was so controversial that Anna Freud blocked its publication for several years.

15 Freud commented that speech in dreams was less frequent and often represented something heard during the day.

16 He wrote this masterpiece after writing the *Commentary* in his mid-twenties (Halbertal, op. cit.).

17 About half the laws relate to activities such as sacrifice within the Temple, which was destroyed some 11 centuries earlier. That is, Maimonides chose to be complete about explicating all the laws, including those that we could no longer perform since the Temple's destruction. The physical place was in ruins; the laws he kept alive.

18 Other words for "law" include "*chok*" (an unexplained law) and "*mitzvah*" (from *tzavah*, command). The latter contains a military component. In contemporary Hebrew, for instance, the *Tzavah* is the Israeli army. In that sense, the Hebrews are often referred to as God's army.

19 Maimonides distinguishes different types of "law." Here, he uses the Arabic "*fiqh*," the "true science of the law that is what man is out to *think and believe*" (rather than only behave) (Strauss, op. cit.) (Szajnberg's italics added).

20 There may be hidden wisdom in the root of *Halacha*; here, as with Aristotle, is a form of the peripatetic.

21 I thank Sandor Gilman for this brief summary of psychoanalysis as well as his commentary throughout this paper.

22 Freud's detailed associations to the Irma dream will be covered in the chapter on Freud's Irma dream.

23 This tale is predated in the Book of Ruth, albeit more delicately. Ruth's husband dies, leaving her childless. Like Tamar, she dresses up to seduce Boaz, a relative (like Judah). Her offspring, most famously, is Jesse, David's father. That is, both in Tamar/Judah and in Ruth/Boaz, infertility is remedied by a pseudo incest (an extension of Leverite marriage) and the forerunners of King David, a great redeemer of the Jewish nation and a man who transgresses further by wedding Bathsheva after purposely sending her husband to die in battle. The sexual boundary violations are continued by King David, who infamously sent Batsheva's husband into battle and sure death in order to bed her. From them, after a (punitive) stillbirth, arose King Solomon.

24 Meltzer's *Philosophy Between the Lines: The Lost History of Esoteric Writings* (2014) is a panoramic sweeping perspective on esoteric (i.e., hidden/revealing) writing from the time of *Bible* and *Plato* until about the early eighteenth century, when, as Goethe lamented, secretive/hidden writing was abandoned, even abhorred in liberal, democratic societies, even as it continues to be used both in totalitarian regimes and, more subtly, in academic disciplines and democratic societies. He cites Leo Strauss, who escaped the Nazi regime, for recognizing the degree to which hidden/revealed writing has been used in the past and the four different motivations for such writing between the lines and hence the importance of learning how to read between the lines to understand the author's honest intent. That is, per Strauss, serious writing is written in layers, a concept familiar to psychoanalysts.

25 Strauss offers as an example how Maimonides, a scholar of Aristotle, first quotes Aristotle and later repeats the quote with a meaningful omission that reverses the meaning of Aristotle, a reversal that accords with Maimonides' 'meaning.

26 Of course, in Hebrew, the word gender is changed with Rachel and Joseph.

27 That is, a recurrent *Torah* theme that something appears bad for an individual, but is good for the Jewish people.

28 As noted earlier, Erikson wrote a scholarly paper on the value of elucidating the manifest content so that it adds to our interpretation of the latent material (Erikson, 1954).

29 While Maimonides was well-regarded by many in the Jewish community, he was criticized and assaulted by the *Gaonic* rabbis, including the prominent Nahmanides. For instance, Maimonides stated (citing *Torah*) that neither rabbis nor yeshivas should charge for studying or teaching about Judaism (!). This threatened the livelihoods of many rabbis and their schools.

30 Maimonides' family had to escape Andalusia, their home, and refuge after the Moorish invasion and forced conversion of Jews. They lived in the Maghreb, again facing anti-Jewish pressure. Then in Egypt, he now faced excommunication from fellow Jews for his writings. That is, Maimonides experienced pressure from Islamic rulers and fellow Jewish rabbis (specifically, the conservative *Gaonim*) for his ideas and writings.

31 An example of an opinion that the other rabbis found egregious was Maimonides' insistence that Jewish leaders (specifically rabbis and *yeshivas*) *should not accept money for their Jewish work*. Maimonides backed his opinion with quotes from the Talmud among other sources.

32 Bakan (1975) claims that somehow Freud was influenced by Maimonides work but gives no evidence for this. Bakan and colleagues (Bakan et. al 2009) published a later text arguing that Maimonides' work somehow influenced Freud's education, without providing evidence for the latter. Tirosh (2011) provides an astute review of the circular reasoning in that a text.

33 Very Orthodox schools teach not only a page of Talmud each day, but also a page of Maimonides.

34 The *geniza* were repositories in the attics of old Egyptian synagogues where many old texts and letters were deposited rather than discarded. This was done out of concern that the real name of God, unknown to man, might by chance be written in one of these scraps and therefore should not be discarded.

35 An intriguing speculation by Halbertal (op. cit.) is that had the family fled to Provençal with many other Jews, and their fate might have been softened by the more tolerant political powers. Halbertal gives a complex explanation of why Jews fleeing to the Maghreb, the center of Moorish power, were somewhat more favorably treated than those who remained in Andalusia. This takes us beyond the reach of this paper.

36 This was not a theoretical argument. At that time, some Ashkenazi (northern European) Jewish communities, Jews—supported by their rabbis—were committing suicide rather than convert (Halbertal, op. cit.).

37 Maimonides insisted that rabbis and yeshivas should not accept money for their work. This, likely, did not make him popular with his colleagues.

38 For instance, we recall the first two of Maimonides' 13 principles for Judaism: the unity of God and his incorporeality *(nimtzah)*, which may also be translated as non-appearing). For a moment, let us consider what Maimonides says about God to be applied to ourselves: that is, Maimonides discovers that we are one, not multiple selves; that our souls/psyche appears immaterial, but compelling. I realize that for someone Orthodox Jewish, this may be

unacceptable. But, for scholars, this is a consideration, a translation of Maimonides concepts from "polytheism" to monotheism, or in our terms, from multiple impulses/selves to a one self who struggles with the various impulses.

References

Anzieu Didier (1986). *Freud's Self-Analysis: Translated from the French by Peter Graham. With a Preface by M. Masud R. Khan IPA Library.* International Universities Press
Auchinclass, E. and Samberg, E. (2012). *Psychoanalytic Terms and Concepts.* Yale.
Auerbach, E. (1954). *Mimesis: Representation of Reality in Western Literature.* Princeton.
Bakan, D. (1975). *Sigmund Freud and the Jewish Mystical Tradition.* Penguin.
Bakan, D., Merkur, D., and Weiss, D. (2009). *Maimonides' Cure of Souls: Medieval Precursor of Psychoanalysis.* SUNY.
Blechner, M. J. (2013). What Are Dreams Like and How Does the Brain Make Them That Way? *Contemp. Psychoanal.*, 49(2):165–175.
Bloom, H. (2004). *Where Shall Wisdom Be Found.* Riverhead.
Durkheim, E. (1987). *The Elementary Forms of Religious Life.* Oxford.
Eiliade, M. (1987). *The Sacred and the Profane.* Harcourt.
Erikson, E. H. (1954). The Dream Specimen of Psychoanalysis. *JAPA*, 2:5–56.
Fishbane, M. (2003). *Biblical Mythmaking and Rabbinic Mythmaking.* Oxford.
Freud, S. (1900). *The Interpretation of Dreams.* SE II. pp. 223–224.
Freud, S. (1917). *Mourning and Melancholia.* S. E. Volume XIV (1914–1916): On the History of the Psycho-Analytic Movement, Papers on Metapsychology and Other Works, pp. 237–258.
Freud, S. (1939). *An Outline of Psychoanalysis New York:.* W. W. Norton & Co., Inc, 1949. Goethe, 1840-1 Faust Part I, Scene 4 Lines 1840-1.
Gay, P. (1998). *Freud: A Life for Our Times.* Norton.
Gilman, S. (2020). Personal Communication.
Giovacchini, P. (1971). Characterological Factors in Creativity. *JAPA*, 19(3):524–542.
Halbertal, M. (2007). *Concealment and Revelation.* Princeton.
Halbertal, M. (2014). *Maimonides: Life and Thought.* Princeton.
Harrari, Y. (2014). *Sapiens: A Brief History of Humankind.* Harper.
Klein, Y. (1968). *Lecture for NCD on Aristotle's Man.* University of Chicago.
Kris, E. (1950). On Preconscious Mental Processes. *Psychoanal. Q*, 19:540–560.
Lerner, R. (2000). *Maimonides' Empire of Light.* University of Chicago Press.
Maimoindes, Iggeret Temani in Lerner (2000). *Maimonides Empire of Light* pp. 14–27/U of Chicago Press.
Maimonides.' *The Guide of the Perplexed.* (1963). Trans., Shlomo Pines. Chicago.
Makari, G. (2008). *Revolution in Mind: The Creation of Psychoanalysis.* Norton.
Makari, G. (2015). *Soul Machine: The Invention of the Modern Mind.* Norton.
Meltzer, A. (2014). *Philosophy Between the Lines: The Lost History of Esoteric Writings. University of Chicago Press.*
Reik, T. (1983). *The Third Ear.* Farrar.
Richards, A. (2022). Freud's Jewish Identity. *International Journal of Psychoanalytic Controversies.* Fall.
Ricoeur, P. (1977). *Freud and Philosophy.* Yale.
Stern, J. (2013). *Maimonides: Matter and Form.* Harvard.

Stimmel, B. (1996). New Directions in Dream Interpretation edited by Gayle Delaney Albany: State University of New York Press, *1993, vi* + 308 pp., $18.95 Paper. *Psa. Books*, 7(1):77–81.

Strauss, L. (1952). *Persecution and the Art of Writing.* Glencoe Free Press.

Strauss, L. (1960). Introduction to Maimonides' Guide of the Perplexed. In *Leo Strauss, Writings on Maimonides.* U. Of Chicago Press.

Strauss, L. (2013). *Leo Strauss on Maimonides: The Complete Writings.* University of Chicago Press.

Strunk, W. and White, E. B. (2005). *Elements of Style.* Penguin.

Szajnberg, N. (1992). Psychoanalysis as an Extension of Autobiographical Genre: Poetry and Truth, Fiction and Reality. *Int. J. Psychoanal.*, 19(3):375–387.

Szajnberg, N. (1996). Towards a Conceptual Alliance about Therapeutic Alliance: A Voyage Through the Inferno. *J. Am. Acad. Psa*, 24(1):95–113.

Szajnberg, N. (1997). The Aesthetic Aspects of Psychoanalysis. *J. Am. Acad. Psa*, 25(2): 189–210.

Szajnberg, N. (2018). *Jacob and Joseph, Judaism's Architects and Birth of the Ego Ideal.* Cambridge Scholars.

Szajnberg, N. (2010). Dante's *Commedia*: Its Contribution to a Psychoanalytic Sense of What Is Human and Precursors of Psychoanalytic Technique. *Int. J. Psychoanal*, 91:183–197.

Szajnberg, N. (2011). Clarity and Ambiguity in Psychoanalytic Practice. *Bull. Menn. Clin.*, 75(1):1–20.

Tirosh,-Samuelson, H. (2011). *Book Review of: Maimonides' Cure of Soul: Medieval Precursor of Psychoanalysis.* Bakan, D. Merkur, D. Weiss, D. SUNY 2009 In H-Judaica.

Wax, M. (1997). Personal communication.

Chapter 2

Rambam: B'reishit ("In the Beginning"; or "At the Head"[1])

The reader should expect a psychoanalyst to display some knowledge, even understanding of Maimonides' early life and later vicissitudes that lay the foundation for his two major constructions, two great "cathedrals" to Judaism, the *Mishnah Torah* and *The Guide of the Perplexed*. I rely on Halbertal's scholarly, award-winning account for much of the biographical information (Halbertal, 2014). Having read about the *Mishnah Torah* in our last chapter, and before we turn to his *Guide* begun some decade later, let us recount his life and how this life leads to the *Guide*.

The eldest son of two born in 1138 into a scholarly Andalusian family, the radical Islam Almohads drove his family in 1148 (when he was ten) from Cordoba, the family initially settling in Seville, then in Morocco's Maghrib. To give a sense of the profound loss to the Jewish community, prior to the Almohad invasion, Andalusia was the birthplace of such revered Jewish poets as Shmuel Hanagid, Solomon bin Gabirol, Moses Ibn Ezra, Yehudah Halevi, and Abraham Ibn Ezra. It was Halevi (1075–1141), however, who wrote the yearning poignant poem:

לִבִּי בְמִזְרָח וְאָנֹכִי בְּסוֹף מַעֲרָב
אֵיךְ אֶטְעֲמָה אֵת אֲשֶׁר אֹכַל וְאֵיךְ יֶעֱרָב
אֵיכָה אֲשַׁלֵּם נְדָרַי וֶאֱסָרַי, בְּעוֹד
צִיּוֹן בְּחֶבֶל אֱדוֹם וַאֲנִי בְּכֶבֶל עֲרָב
יֵקַל בְּעֵינַי עֲזֹב כָּל טוּב סְפָרַד, כְּמוֹ
יֵקַר בְּעֵינַי רְאוֹת עַפְרוֹת דְּבִיר נֶחֱרָב.

My heart is in the East and I at the end of the West/
How can I taste what I eat, and how I go/
How to fulfill my vows and my prohibitions, while/
Zion is in bloodied rope and I in Arab chains./
It would be light in my eyes to leave all good in Spain, If
My eyes could see the dust of our ruined holy place.

(Author's translation)

Maimoinides' father was a judge in the Jewish court. Maimonides could trace his family back seven generations to Jerusalem. Even after three

DOI: 10.4324/9781003358213-2

decades living in Egypt, Maimonides referred to himself as "the Spaniard" or the "Andalusian" (Halbertal, op cit). While Maimonides father was his primary teacher, Maimonides referred to his father's teachers, rabbis Isaac Alfasi and Joseph Halevi bin Migash, as his own teachers.

Maimonides spent seven years writing his *Commentary* on the Mishnah, completing it in 1168 (at 30) while, exiled, roaming through Maghreb and completing it in Egypt. Even before he started the *Commentary*, Maimonides was recognized by scholars as a "great sage" (Ibn Aknin, *Perush le-Shir ha-Shirim*, p. 398; Halbertal, op. cit.). Halbertal persuades us of the impact of Maimonides' exile from Andalusia:

> "A traumatic event of personal and cultural loss ... it set the perception of crisis within which he worked.... Maimonides' life can be seen ... as an effort to preserve and reconstruct his homeland ... to save the Jewish world from the *halakhic* and spiritual ruin he had experienced."
>
> (p. 23)

Intriguingly, one major *halakhic* disagreement against Maimonides was made by rabbis who prohibited Jews from sailing on Babylonian Rivers during Shabbat. Maimonides defended this; we can at least wonder to what degree he was thinking of his brother, who supported his family and Maimonides with international shipping.

In his letters, Maimonides reveals his connection to Aristotle via his study of Arabic neo-Aristotilians (Halbertal, p. 21; p. 136). "Aristotle reached the highest levels of knowledge ... with the exception of one who experiences the emanation of the Divine Spirit..." We will see how *The Guide* attempts to elevate his student, Joseph, to a higher level than Aristotle's.

Maghreb (1159–1166) was no refuge. During Maimonides' sojourn, during the time he wrote his *Commentary*, the Almohads killed Jews who refused to convert to Islam, kidnapped their children, confiscated Jewish estates, and made Jews wear marked clothing (Halbertal, p. 25).

When we read of the rabbinical fuss over sailing on Shabbat on the Tigris or Euphrates, we are diverted, almost, from the more life-threatening issues of Islamic forced conversion or death. Maimonides wrote an *Epistle on Martyrdom*, insisting that "conversion" under threat of death was not real conversion: that Torah (Deuteronomy 30:19) insists "I have set before you life and death,... choose life, that both thou and thy seed may live." One wonders what they were thinking, debating fiercely over boats on Shabbat, when lives were hanging at the end of Almohad's ropes.[2] Still, Maimonides addressed lives to be lived, and strongly recommended that the threatened Jews in exile move again, as he had. The persecuted Jew should "...leave everything he has ... travel day and night ... to where he can practice his religion" (Halbertal, *Epistle*, p. 31–2).

In 1166, now 28, Maimonides, his father, brother, and the family moved to Jerusalem, where he reflects fondly years later, "...(we) walked through the House of the Lord with great feeling" (Halbertal, op. cit. *Iggeret*, p. 230). Faced with poverty, the family instead moved to Egypt, first Fustat (outside Cairo) then Alexandria, and back to Fustat. Maimonides' father died shortly after the move.

Maimonides married in his early thirties, late for that era, but consistent with his values that sexual passion is secondary to a passion for wisdom and knowledge of God. Maimonides quotes Aristotle on the sense of touch "as a disgrace" (Halbertal, op. cit.137–140), although Leo Strauss suggests that the quoted fragment from Aristotle is reversed when the final two words are added. In fact, this is an example, per Strauss of Maimonides' technique of "hiding" his true meaning by using omission (Strauss, 1963). Maimonides shows his understanding of human nature when he cautions that illicit intercourse is hard to resist (Halbertal, p. 37). His son, Abraham, was born in 1186 (Maimonides now 48) and a daughter was born and died afterward.

By 1171, five years after moving to Egypt, Maimonides was selected as head of the Jewish community, *ra'is al-yahud*. This prestigious political appointment also brought opprobrium: "...in Egypt. Illness and material loss overwhelmed me. Informers plotted against my life" (Letters of Maimonides, p. 72). He reciprocated with critiques: referring to those who called themselves *rosh yeshiva* (*yehiva* head), or *av bet din* (chief judge, literarily, "father of the court"), Maimonides said that many did not have "learning (equal) to one who has been in the study hall only one day" (*Commentary on the Mishnah Behkorot* 4:4). Perhaps Maimonides' most provocative act was to insist that yeshivas or rabbis not get money for Jewish study: study is payment in itself; rabbis should have day jobs (as did Maimonides, as a physician) (Avot, 4:7). Because the *ra'is al-yehud* is a political appointment (from both Muslim rulers and the Jewish community), it was vulnerable to "intrigue bribery and struggle (Halbertal, pp. 44–46); Maimonides was deposed after two years by someone he regarded as a political hack (in his words, "contemptible and morally impoverished...") (*Iggerot*, p. 450).

Maimonides' *Epistle to Yemen* (1172) was an intellectual hallmark written in response to Yemenite rabbis' pleas for advice and help because of the onslaught of Islam and astrology and Messiahs in Yemen threatening the Jewish community, We are given a sense of the geographical breadth of Moslem threats against the exiled Jewish communities ranging from Maimonides' Andalusia (and Provence) eastward to Yemen. Maimonides responds by recasting Jewish history as prophesied by Daniel. There are the following three stages of threats to Jewish belief and existence:

First, armed attack on Jews
Second, arguments to undermine Jewish faith
Third (and most insidious), imitation of Jewish beliefs to sow doubt
   and confusion

Maimonides offers some solace based on Daniel's vision of four beasts: ultimately the Jews will prevail over the Christians (who accept the Torah as authoritative but whose Trinity opposes the unity of God) and Moslems (who consider the Torah as forgery, yet have a unitary God). Cold comfort perhaps to the Yemenite Jews. Yet, Maimonides was concerned that this letter, which he asked to be read at public gatherings—as in Ezra's time— would jeopardize him. Nevertheless, he insisted, ". public welfare takes precedence over one's personal safety" (ibid, p. 131). This *Epistle* falls in the category of highly *exo*teric; no secret messages are buried here.

Mishnah Torah

We dedicate a chapter to *Mishnah Torah* in this book, but in terms of Maimonides' life, it is in this decade (1168–1177) that he completes this work of a thousand chapters (Halbertal, 2014). Supported by his brother David's international and hazardous import/export business, Maimonides "labored day and night" to complete this compilation of all the Commandments and overview of commentaries (*Iggerot*, p. 542–3).

David's drowning death in 1177 along with most of the families' assets on the Indian Ocean abruptly terminated this phase of Maimonides' life (he was then 49). We suggest here and develop later in this book, the profound loss and mourning catalyzed his decision to write the deeply enigmatic, esoteric *Guide*, a study for those "perplexed" by the apparent antinomies of *Torah* and "science" (i.e., Aristotelian science). Or, those perplexed by the *Job* story and its reconciliation with God's providence for man; *Job* shifts us from eye-for-an-eye punishment, from rewards for living the *mitzvoth*, to a more challenging view of how to live one's life, a more challenging sense of how to reach for God with both wisdom and passion.

Some years before, David confessed the dangers of his voyages in a letter to Maimonides; Maimonides admonished David not to take on such perilous journeys.

How affected Maimonides was by his brother's death we hear in Maimonides' own words:

> "For almost a year … I lay on my couch stricken with fever, despair, and *on the brink of destruction.*"
>
> (Letters, p. 74; italics added by this author)

Hear Maimonides eight years after David's death:

> "…I still mourn for him for there can be no consolation. … He grew up on my knees, he was my brother, my pupil. He went abroad to trade that I might remain at home and continue my studies. He was well versed in Talmud and Torah and an accomplished grammarian. My greatest joy

was to see him. Now, *every joy has been dimmed*. He has departed to his eternal life and left me confounded in a strange land. Whenever I come across his handwriting on one of his books, *my heart turns within me and my grief reawakens*.

(Letters of Maimonides, p. 73; Halbertal, 2018; author's italics).

This sweep of grief is compelling. But two phrases give us pause that might enlighten his soon-to-be *Guide*.

First, his phrase that he feels "confounded in a strange land ..." brings to mind Maimonides' citation from *Torah* when he was deciding to name his new book as "perplexed." Gesundheit and Hadad (2021)[3] Exodus 14:3 says that the desert-wandering Israelites were *"nevukhim b'aretz,"* perplexed in the land. Maimonides even cited this phrase in choosing the title of his book. His feeling "confounded" after his brother's tragic death may have captured the sense of lostness or perplexedness of the Israelites in their 40 years of desolate wandering.

Second, we suggest further that Maimonides *explicitly* dedicated his *Guide* to only one student who left prematurely, Joseph; *implicitly*, he may be dedicating it to another "student" who left prematurely, David. After all, in Maimonides' own words, "...he was my brother, *my pupil*." The explicit and implicit in Maimonides are imbricated.

Maimonides' enduring and deep mourning runs counter not only to Jewish law, but also to Maimonides own commentary of that law in his *Mishnah Torah (Laws of Mourning, 13:11)*. Maimonides quotes *Jeremiah 22:10: "Weep not for the dead, neither bemoan him."* Even for a deeply rational scholar as Maimonides, his brother's death outweighs Maimonides' knowledge of Law, which teaches us that heavy feeling tips the scale of humanity.

Hear the personal circumstances, the matrix within which Maimonides was immersed when writing the *Guide*. Begun around 1190 and completed around 1199, his Arabic manuscript was sent to Ibn Tibbon in Provence to translate into Hebrew. Maimonides reviewed the translation as it progressed until it was completed and published several days before his death. That is, we can rely on the Hebrew translation's accuracy as approved by Maimonides.

After David's death in 1177, Maimonides turned to medical practice in 1178, which he had studied in Morocco. In 1191, Maimonides was appointed physician to the vizier to Saladin. He practiced in Cairo into the night, often having to recline from exhaustion while he did consultations, and returning home to Fustat. He lamented that he no longer had time to study Torah, except on Shabbat.

He also took on his special student, Joseph ben Judah, from Morocco, who grabbed Maimonides' attention by sending a rhymed successful appeal to study with Maimonides (Halbertal, 2014). And "study" meant learning astronomy, mathematics, and logic to prepare for metaphysics. This is the student to whom Maimonides dedicated the series of missives called the *Guide*, this "book" that Maimonides refused to call a book.

A brother's drowning death, financial strain, new familial responsibilities, tutoring a prize student from afar, practicing as a physician into waning hours, the political vicissitudes of *ra'is al-yehud*, desperate pleas for advice from far-flung Jewish communities—all these were the medium within which Maimonides was immersed when he chose to compose this purposely complex, perplexing, intentionally concealing yet revealing text that is the *Guide*.

However, Maimonides' ten-year toil in his twenties that resulted in the 14-volume *Mishneh Torah* was a foundation for the *Guide* written a decade later. While the *Mishneh Torah* is considered an exoteric text—clear, transparent, in Hebrew—Strauss calls it paradoxically the most *eso*teric of exoteric texts. Grasping a sense of the Mishneh Torah prepares us for the leap that is the Guide. Before leaping, let us step into this preparatory landscape, just as Moses surveyed the Land of Israel from Qades*h Barneah*.

Notes

1   Embedded in the first word of the Torah, 'בראשית' "be'reishit" is the word ראש, "rosh" 'head." Hence the play on words. In the beginning, so to speak, in Hebrew, the world is started in God's "head.").

2   This reminds us of the 1938 text, *Aesthetics and Politics* by Walter Benjamin, Adorno, Bloch, Lukacs, and Brecht, heatedly debating whether Expressionism will endure, Benjamin spouting his idiosyncratic "Marxist" perspective (He, who had been rejected by the Marxists). This while the Nazi scourge was threatening their lives; not a word was written about the threats to their existence in this last book with Benjamin's published final words. The Introduction begins, "The conflict between Ernst Bloch and Georg Lukacs over expressionism in 1938 forms *one of the most revealing episodes in modern German letters.*" (Italics added by NS.) 1938! Revealing, yes, although not in the sense that that author intended. Really, what *were* they thinking?

3   I thank Josef Stern for this citation and his equally useful "Shlomo Pines on the Translation of Maimonides' Guide of the Perplexed" (Kraemer and Stern, 1998).

References

Gesundheit, B. and Hadad, E. (2021). The Guide of the Perplexed—What's in a Name. *Rev. des études Juives*, 180(1–2):191–205.

Halbertal, M. (2014a). Maimonides. Princeton.

Halbertal, M. (2014b). Maimonides, Ibn Aknin, *Perush le-Shir ha-Shirim*, p. 398.

Kraemer, J. and Stern, J. (1998). Shlomo Pines on the Translation of Maimonides' Guide of the Perplexed. *J. Jew. Thought Philos.*, 8:13–24.

Strauss L. (1963). Introduction to Maimonides Guide of the Perplexed. Transl. Pines. U of Chicago Press.

Chapter 3

Mishnah Torah

Precedence for *The Guide* (מורה נבוכים); *Historical Context*

The Guide wasn't Maimonides' first esoteric "rodeo." Halbertal (2014) demonstrates persuasively that Maimonides' youthful *Mishnah Torah*, (Maimonides, trans. Hyamson, 1937) written over a decade beginning in his twenties, is known primarily as an *exoteric* text, a clear explanation of the 613 Laws. Yet, Maimonides buries ambiguity both in the title of the book and more so in how he wrote it; he wraps hidden meanings of the entire work within its overt portrayal as a book of explanation.

First the title, *Mishnah Torah*. Hebrew readers will know that the *Torah* comes from the word "learning," implying that it is a text for learning (how to live one's life). The reader will also hear the same "root" in Maimonides' מורה נבוכים, *Moreh Nevuchim*, or *The Guide*: *Moreh* and *Torah* are almost homonyms which share the root associated with the meaning of "הוראה," "teaching." Given that Maimonides was meticulous with word choice, he would have carefully selected his title: we can at least allow that he intended to echo "*Torah*" in his "*Moreh*"; that his work (modestly) follows the *Torah* as a form of learning/study. As we discuss in more detail in Chapter 4, even the contrast or complement of masculine *Moreh* with feminine *Torah is meaningful*, even critical for Maimonides for us to understand.

The first *Mishnah*, compiled/edited around second century CE by Yehuda HaNassi (Judah the Prince), intended to take the volumes of back and forth of the Oral Torah and condense them into a single work. *Mishnah* can be translated as "re-view" or study (with repetition) or even "re-turn" or turning back to (the *Torah*).[1] A further tone of ambiguity is that *Mishnah* comes from the root שניה "sh'ni'ah," which can also mean "secondary," suggesting that this text is secondary to the primary *Torah*. Of course: implied in Yehuda HaNassi's title is that his book takes the rabbinical debate in the previous two centuries and tries to return to the original meanings in the *Torah*. HaNassi's impetus for writing down what had been traditionally transmitted orally was that the severe crises in Jewish communities and life since their exile from their homeland (initially in the sixth century BCE by the Babylonians, more successfully by the Romans following 70 CE) jeopardized the transmission of knowledge by word of mouth.

DOI: 10.4324/9781003358213-3

Maimonides drew parallels to the vicissitudes of his Jewish world. Personally, he was exiled from his beloved Spain to the Magreb, to Palestine, finally settling in Egypt and overtly thriving there, although his brother's drowning set him back profoundly. Rabbis from around the Middle East and Europe sent questions in distress over how to respond to societal Jewish crises: forced conversions with death threats or expulsion, self-proclaimed messiahs, and resurgence of astrology beliefs. The Jewish communities were threatened. The Jews got conflicting advice from local rabbis: for instance, some rabbis insisted that a Jew faced with forced conversion should choose death; Maimonides disagreed and offered *Torah*-based reasoning to "choose life, so that you and your seed may live" (*Deuteronomy 30:19*. Alter, 2019). And Maimonides believed that the Jewish communities' crises were in part a fallout from the now-centuries of exile. Writing down knowledge about *Torah*, despite its partial prohibition, was necessary to safeguard the Jewish community. In addition to his letters of response, he compiled several books on Jewish matters (before his medical texts in the latter part of his life). The two better known were the *Mishnah Torah* early in his life and *The Guide*, after his brother's death, in the latter part of his life. In order to set a foundation for understanding *The Guide,* let's look more carefully at the voluminous *Mishnah Torah*.

The title, we suggest, is both clear and ambiguously evasive (Strauss, 2013; Halbertal, 2014). The word *Mishnah* could be a modest homage to the great Yehuda HaNassi's *Mishnah*, or "return." The full title, *Mishnah Torah*, could be heard humbly as a return to the *Torah*, the foundational *Five Books of Moses*, the first book of that triumvirate acronymed *Ta'na'ch* (*Torah, Nevi'im, Ketuvim; Five Books of* Moses*, the Prophets, the Writings*). In that sense, the *Mishnah Torah* lightly skips over the multivocal, even garrulous, dissonant Babylonian or Jerusalem *Talmuds*, with their heated (Hillel vs. Shammai) rabbinical debates, and with some certitude, Maimonides skips over the subsequent post-Talmud *Ge'onim and Amor'im* or local rabbis' opinions that might hold for their own communities (Yemen, or Provence) but may not be accepted as Law by the overall Jewish Community.[2] Maimonides' *Mishnah Torah* elides the dozens of rabbinical asides, disagreements, expositions in Talmud, or skitters like a flat rock skipping over the ocean's waves over the bickering rabbis: for each of the 613 Commandments/Laws, Maimonides offers a singular clarification of its meaning (and hence how to live one's life accordingly). That is, this title, *Mishnah Torah*, can be a modest "re-turn," a parabolic soaring over the centuries of commentaries, to the *Torah*. Or more provocatively, it adroitly sidesteps several generations *and* contemporary rabbis, post *Talmud,* and even one-ups the multifocal, at times quibbling chorus of *Talmud* arguments to bring some clarity to the original 613 Commandments. Maimonides' attitude toward the *Talmud*— sidestepping the fractious debates and at times its contended decisions,—differs, for instance, when Talmudic decisions are made on the basis of "magical" beliefs (cf. harm caused by seeing, or *Leverite* marriage; Halbertal, 2014, p. 257 ff). Being lean, Maimonides is judgmental: *this* shall be included, *that* shall not. Inherent in selection is a judgment of what is closer to the original *Torah* and what can be, well … set aside. Halbertal points out that Maimonides even left ambiguous whether the *Mishnah Torah* should be "only" a commentary on *Halachah*[3] … or intended to be *Halacha* itself, a bolder, even presumptuous stance.

Let's for the moment telescope out historically to see how Maimonides' *Mishnah Torah* sits among the constellations of commentaries on *Torah*. The *Five Books of Moses*, the *Torah*, is the primary text of the Jewish people, recounting the 613 Laws on how to live one's life. About half of these are Laws for the Temple, Laws which became dormant once the temple was destroyed the second time by the Romans. The second and third holy texts that follow are the *Prophets* (including Isaiah and importantly for Maimonides, *Ezekiel*) and the *Writings* (e.g., *Song of Songs, Ecclesiastes, and the Ester Story*).

After the Babylonian exile and Babylon's defeat by the Persians (around 600 BCE), the Jews were invited to return to Israel and rebuild the Temple. This is recounted in the Ezra/Nehemiah book. Ezra was the priest/scribe and Nehemiah was the administrator sent to rebuild the Temple. Ezra, concerned about the loss of biblical knowledge, calls the Jewish people together before the "water gate" and recites from a scroll the Five Books of Moses. The Ezra book expresses one of the earliest concerns that the Jewish people might be forgetting the Bible (and its Commandments).

The converse—from Jewish *return* during Persian times *to* Jewish *destruction and two-millennia dispersal* in Roman times—occurred over 600 years later. The Romans toppled the Jewish state (70 CE), destroyed the Temple, killed some 1,100,00 Jews (Josephus, 1984) (Roman horsemen complained that the streets were so deep in Jewish blood that Roman horses had difficulty maneuvering); spread salt on the land so that nothing could grow; and dispersed the Jewish people to the ends of the then-known earth. The Romans even renamed the Jews and their land "Palestinian" to erase their identity. This is how in the mid-second century CE, Yehuda HaNassi inherited the state of the Jewish people and made the first attempt, his *Mishnah*, to compile a summary of the Geonic rabbinical debate, differences over interpreting the Laws in the prior two centuries.[4] HaNassi's conceptual model for the *Mishnah* texts is to divide it into six topics covering six major categories of Laws. These are as follows:

1 *Zeytim* (seeds): prayer, blessings, agricultural laws
2 *Moad* (holidays): sabbath and holidays
3 *Nashim* (women): laws about women, including menses
4 *Nizikin* (damages): culpability for damages (gored by your ox, etc.)
5 *Kodashim* (holiness): rites (for the Temple)
6 *Toharot* (purity): pertaining to sacred (and profane)

Some 1000 years later, Maimonides experiences and sees similar crises among the continued Jewish exile, expulsions and dispersion, and forced conversions (by *both* Christianity and Islam). Like HaNassi, he tries to summarize in writing (here, in Hebrew primarily, occasionally Aramaic, the *Talmud's* tongue) the interpretations of the Laws. But he follows a unique model: he starts (and finishes) with knowledge of God (Halbertal, 2014). This is critical for not only his *Mishnah Torah,* but also over a decade later for his pinnacle text, *The Guide of the Perplexed.* He also ends his *Mishnah Torah* with knowledge of God. Without further details for now, suffice to say that for Maimonides, "knowledge" of God is not simply an intellectual (or "philosophical") affair: it includes the emotion "awe"[5] (as a category beyond "fear") and the emotions associated with awe, which for him includes or allies with the love of God. The ultimate aim, for Maimonides, is to live a good Jewish life via striving to love/be in awe of God: to identify with His knowledge, even to follow His ways of governing. This is an asymptotic goal, we will learn, for Maimonides, a lifetime effort that is reminiscent of Aristotle's view of man as a hopping being, episodically reaching the heavens (through man's critical inquiry and thought) and being hauled back to earth by life's gravity (Klein, 1968). But for Maimonides, man is bound to earth by the gravity of his flesh's needs and desires (Stern, 2013).

Maimonides' *Mishnah Torah* has 14 divisions. The first, the aforementioned *"Book of Knowledge"* starts with the terms for God, followed by chapters on divinity, the universe, and chapters on Ezekiel's Chariot and the Creation. (The latter two become the *only* topics of interest in his later *Guide*: the Creation represents the study of physics; the Chariot, the study of Metaphysics.) In his *Mishnah Torah*, Maimonides is clear that *the* goal of following the Laws is "realizing one's perfection.... the actualization of a person's potential (for).... A creature possessed of understanding" (Halbertal, 2014, p. 197). In the phrase "creature possessed of understanding," we hear an echo of Aristotle's description of man as a "rational animal," an animal, but (potentially) infused with understanding (Aristotle's phrase was "rational principle" (λόγον ἔχον)[6] (Aristotle, *Nicomachean Ethics I.13; or "deliberative imagination" (*Aristotle, *De anima III.11)*).

Let's look for the moment at Maimonides' foundation for the 14 books of *Mishnah Torah* before we leap several centuries to compare his conceptual framework with Joseph Karo's *Shulkhan Arukh*, another systematic commentary on *Torah* (and the commentaries). Maimonides, in his second chapter, draws a continuum with two major leaps, from love and *fear* of God, via contemplation to love and *awe* of God. *Halachah* is the "walking path" of this life times' effort. Maimonides demonstrates an astute understanding of the difference between the emotions of 'fear" and "awe" (Ekman, 2000): fear is a more fundamental emotion; we can say "primitive," trembling before someone so powerful as God. Via the path of the hunger for more knowledge about this God, fear shifts to the more sophisticated and humble "awe," a sense of smallness before the greatness of the universe and its Creator. "The pinnacle of the religious experience is the joining of love and awe" (Halbertal, 2014, p. 199). Maimonides, that dual devotee of religion and science, concludes:

"I shall explain some large, general aspects of the Works of the Sovereign of the Universe, that they may serve the intelligent individual as a door to the love of God" (Maimonides, 1963, 2:2).

Maimonides cites *Torah*, astutely attentive to his rabbinical colleagues, science-averse, skeptical: "Observe the Universe and hence you will know Him who spoke and the world was" (op. cit. 2:2).

To amplify the conceptual distinction between Maimonides' organization of *Mishnah Torah* and others, we look at Karo's *Shulkhan Arukh* in the sixteenth century (another time of fervent tumult including the exile of Jews from the Iberian peninsula by King Ferdinand and Queen Isabella). Karo's name for his commentaries on the Bible sets his stage: the *Shulkhan Arukh*, or Table of Order, or Prepared Table. His book will be organized temporally. Laws emerge by the time of day: upon arising, a man says the following prayers; at dusk (when the raven's wing cannot be distinguished from the night), the evening prayers, and so on. This is a very different organizing principle from Maimonides' beginning (and ending) with knowledge of God, or the earlier HaNassi's attempt to cluster the Laws by six categories of prayers, damages, women, through purity.

Let's return to Maimonides' *Mishnah Torah* to understand how it contains the seeds of *The Guide,* both conceptually and in Maimonides' germination from *predominately* exoteric to *predominately* esoteric. Maimonides argues that to serve God from love one must possess the following four characteristics:

1 To *know* (study the Laws)
2 To *act* properly (fulfill the Commandments)
3 To *walk* in wisdom
4 To have *pure motives* (non-transactional)

Maimonides turns to the *Prophets* to argue that to know, to recite, to say just the words, or perform the rituals, can be empty acts. One must live one's life in accordance with the Laws.

And, here is a new controversial contribution. *Deuteronomy*—Moses' final words to the Israelites about how to live properly—has a transactional nature—do good, be rewarded; do bad, be punished—eye for eye/tooth for tooth. Challenging this, Maimonides argues (citing *Isaiah* and others) if one serves God out of love annealed with awe (following the four principles above), one becomes impelled by no external motive:" .... neither by fear of calamity nor ... desire to obtain material benefits ... happiness comes to him as a result of his conduct" (Maimonides, *Laws Concerning Repentance*, 1937 10:1-2).

Only some decades later in his *Guide* does Maimonides confess that such internal non-transactional motivation may only arise in the elect, the most educated (in both *Torah* and sciences).

Maimonides demonstrates a developmental understanding of human nature: *fear precedes love and awe* (Ekman, 2000; Halbertal, 2014). Love is not transactional. Fear is. Fear may be a necessary first step to follow the Laws. But to reach higher levels of inner nobility (and truer closeness to God), fear is supplanted by love and awe. Intriguingly, "love" is reciprocal (while not transactional), yet "awe" is not transactional nor even reciprocal. Let's explore Maimonides' concept of awe further. Exploring the continuum from fear to awe helps us understand the shift from *Mishneh Torah* to the *Guide*. We take a brief detour to explore these words before returning to *Mishneh Torah* properly.

Awe is a problematic term, in part because we may have a "modern" concept of awe that may not have been present in medieval times. If this is true, it is not unique to English nor Hebrew. Ancient Chinese has no term for "awe." In contemporary Chinese, awe is represented by combining two ideographs: "respect" and "fear."[7] Is this combination, respect/ fear, an accurate representation of Western views of awe, that rare emotion (Ekman, 2000)? Ekman has demonstrated that there are some seven universal emotions; empirically, he expects that we will find some 12 or 13 universal emotions; awe is one of these, but like the noble elements, a rare find.

To understand Maimonides (and *Torah*) on awe, we need to turn to the various Hebrew terms he and *Torah* use. Fear (of God in particular) has one clear term in Biblical/Maimonides' Hebrew: פחד, "*pachad*." But then we have a second term for fear that contains ambiguity of meaning depending on the context. ירא, "*yareh*" is "fear." But in phrases such as ירא אלוהים, yireh *Elohim* (fear/awe of God) (Genesis 22:12) or יראת השמים *yiret hasha- maim* (fear/awe of the sky/heavens), some translators render "yireh/t" as "awe," in this context; others as "fear" (Alter and JPS translate יראת אלוהים as "fear God").

The confound continues as Maimonides links "wisdom" with a shift from "fear" to "awe" of God. He refers to Proverbs 9:10 (attributed to Solomon, hence some centuries later than the Genesis writing). The Hebrew is תחילת חכמה יראת יהוה", *techilat chochmah yirat yehova*" "The beginning of wisdom is fear of *Yehova*" (Alter translation). Maimonides begins to sculpt distinctions within the word "fear" *(yireh)* in the following passage:

"And what is the way of loving Him and fearing Him? When a man reflects upon His wondrous great works and creatures and perceives from them His inestimable and infinite wisdom, he at once loves, praises, glorifies, and yearns greatly to know the Great Name—as David said: My soul thirsts for God, for the living God [Ps 42:3]. And when he mediates on these things themselves, he at once recoils (*nirta'*) in a start, and will fear (*ve-yira'*) and tremble *(ve-yifached)* and know that he is a small *(qetanah)*, lowly *(shfa-lah)*, dark *(a'felah)* creature standing with slight insignificant understanding *(da'at qalah me'uṭah)* before [Him who is] perfect in understanding" (Maimonides, Book of Knowledge, Laws of the Foundations of the Torah 2.2; translated by Ralph Lerner, 2000).

Let's look at the words used by Maimonides, using simpler, more literal translations. Man must undergo the following internal "actions" in order to "love and fear" God: *nirta'* נרתע (recoil), *yirah* ירא (fear), *yifached* יפחד (translated by Lerner as "tremble," but the reader can see the root for *pahad*, פחד "fear," here); and also feel small, lovely, and dark. Only then will we be a "creature" standing with slight insignificant understanding, or literally—for *"da'at qalah me'utah,"* דעת קלה מְעוּטה *a* "knowledge (that is) light/easy/simple and slight." Note that Lerner translates *yirah* as "fear," but *pahad* as "tremble." These are thoughtful decisions by the translator, who nevertheless may lean us unwittingly away from other meanings, including that *yirah* and *pachad* can both be translated as "fear" ... or is *yirah* different? Is *yirah* for Maimonides more akin to "awe" as Pines and Strauss have it (Strauss 1963)?

How does Maimonides explain fear? In a later medical work (On the Regimen of Health (Gerrit Bos, trans. 2019), Maimonides, 2019), Maimonides says that fear is of two psychological origins: 1. The trauma of past loss; 2. Dread of future loss or trauma. Today, from psychoanalytic understanding, we have learned how the two are connected: anticipation or anxiety or fear of future catastrophe *can be* directly connected to past, often early, or deeply traumatic later catastrophes or losses (Winnicott, 1974). We remind ourselves of Maimonides' profound reaction to his brother's untimely drowning death (and the preceding losses associated with being dislocated from his beloved Andalusia). These are not experiences of "awe," but rather, closer to fear. We suggest that there may be for Maimonides a developmental continuum from fear to awe. And we find it in his further writings.

In Guide III, 52, Maimonides puts "fear" and "awe" side by side in this context. When men, like Abraham after the *Akeda*, the near-sacrifice of Isaac, develop "intellectual humility" (Green, 2019), "they achieve such humility, such awe and fear of God, such reverence and shame before Him … in ways that pertain to true reality, not to imagination…." (Maimonides 1963, Pines trans., p. 629).

That is, Maimonides leads us to consider the developmental shift from "fear" to "awe" to be associated with a sense of humility, of our smallness of existence in the world (and even with a sense of shame). We have some shading on the continuum from fear to awe.

Perhaps Maimonides' Judeo-Arabic term for "awe" that he uses in the *Guide*—*yastahiyyu* (يَسْتَحِي) gives us more guidance on his meaning. In contemporary Arabic, it refers to something closer to shame or humbling oneself before making a request.[8]

Maimonides expands on the proper state of mind for "awe" (and wisdom-seeking) in Judeo-Arabic:

"וכד'לך נקול נחן אנה ינבגי ללאנסאן אן לא יתהג'ם להד'א אלאמר אלעט'ים אלג'ליל מן אול והלה
דון אן ירוץ' נפסה פי אלעלום ואלמעארף ויהד'ב אכ'לאקה חק אלתהד'יב ויקתל שהואתה
ותשוקאתה אלכ'יאליה. פאד'א חצל מקדמאת חקיקיה יקיניה ועלמהא ועלם קואנין אלקיאס
ואלאסתדלאל ועלם וג'וה אלתחפט' מן אגאליט אלד'הן חיניד' יקדם ללבחת' פי הד'א אלמעני. ולא
יקטע באול ראי יקע לה ולא ימד אפכארה אולא ויסלטהא נחו אדראך אלאלאה בל יסתחי ויכף
ויקף חתי יסתנהץ' אולא אולא"

In Ibn Tibbon's contemporary Hebrew translation:

"וכן נאמר אנחנו: כי צריך לאדם שלא יהרס לזה העניין העצום הנכבד מתחלת המחשבה בלתי
שירגיל עצמו בחכמות ובדעות, ויזקק מדותיו זקוק רב וימית תאוותיו ותשוקותיו הדמיוניות;
וכאשר יבין הקדמות אמתיות וידעם וידע דרכי ההקש ועשות המופת וידע אפני השמירה מהטעאות
השכל אז יקדים לחקירה בזה העניין; ולא יגזור בתחילת דעת שיעלה בליבו ולא ישלח מחשבותיו
תחילה וישליטם להשגת האלוה אבל יבוש וימנע ויעמוד עד שיעלה ראשון ראשון."

"Let not this vast and respectable matter be destroyed from the beginning of thought unless he exercises himself in wisdom and opinions
and distills his thoughts and needs a lot and kills his imaginary desires
and passions, when he understands true preliminaries and knows and
knows the ways of striking and doing miracles and knows the ways of
guarding against the errors of the mind, then he will advance to the
investigation of this matter; And he will not cut off at the beginning of
a thought that will arise in his heart and will not send his thoughts first
and control them to achieve God, but he will dry up and prevent and
stand until he first comes up first."

Fundamentally, this captures Maimonides' use of "awe": a humbling that
almost approaches self-debasement; one is a small, lowly, dark, insignificant creature. This may not be isotonic with contemporary views of awe
(Ekman, 2000) in that it has more negative self-qualities. The contemporary
sense of awe includes a smallness before the presence of beauty, a religious
experience (without needing to be religious), and a feeling of being moved.
Perhaps Freud's description (Freud, 1929, Freud, 1930) of the oceanic feeling approaches some elements of awe and Freud's lack of such experience.[9]
Freud attributed the oceanic *(la mer)* feeling as a form of unity with early
maternal presence *(la mère)*.

Let's proceed with the *Mishnah Torah*.

Earlier we spoke of the *Mishnah Torah* as *predominately exo*teric. We
are influenced by Strauss's 1937 critical review of a new English translation of Maimonides' volume I of the *Mishnah Torah, Sefer Hamadah,
Book of Knowledge*. Strauss's is a meticulous survey of mistranslations and
outright *censorship by Christian "translators"*[10] of Maimonides. Before I

offer examples, I turn to Strauss's enlightening observation that the *Sefer Hamadah* is "more esoteric than most esoteric works .... (It is) a book of mystery" (Strauss, 2013, p. 329 ff). Strauss opens up the possibility of thinking of the *exoteric-esoteric frame as a continuum* rather than a bipolar dichotomy. Some books are at the far end of the continuum of exoteric, such as the *Odyssey*; others at the far end of *esoteric*, such as Maimonides' *Guide*. Many are between, such as the *Mishnah Torah* (or the *Interpretation of Dreams*, as we will argue later in this book).

There may be a parallel between Strauss's concept of exoteric/esoteric and Auerbach's foreground/background, in which he juxtaposes the *Odyssey's* foreground ("everything" is illuminated, presented) in contrast to the austere Abraham/Isaac *Akeda's* background. These also may be a continuum and may meet at some juncture to a style that captures both background and foreground, or to the inner life (Mendelsohn, 2020; Szajnberg, in press). Further, as we develop in later, with the introduction of psychoanalysis, even exoteric texts may have layered meanings: despite Mark Twain's warning in the preface to Huck Finn that the reader should not seek deeper meanings in the text, the reader *does* gather that the slave Jim is more humanistic than his surrounding slaveholders who hunt him. Like Ishmael and Queequeg in *Moby Dick*, Huck learns much from the less articulate partner in "crime," Jim. For now, let us listen to Strauss and consider that Maimonides' more exoteric *Mishnah Torah* has elements of the esoteric that foretells Maimonides' *Guide*.

A cautionary few words about mistranslations to gird the reader dependent on translations. Maimonides writes:

1 "Words of the wise be few, but meanings many" *(De'ot, VI, 21)*.
2 To teach truth, use secrets, for instance, by contradictory statements[11] (p. 338).
3 Be meticulous about word use, including the careful presentation of ambiguity.
4 Understanding a term, means to understand its context.
5 Therefore, accurate translation is critical for the reader.

Hence, Strauss points out that the new (1942/2018) translation of Volume I of *MT (Maimonides, translated by Hyamson 1937)* was critical as it was based on the handwritten manuscript in the Bodleian library,[12] signed by Maimonides. We discover that Christian censors removed "Jesus" from the original manuscript. We learn how they mistranslated Maimonides' terms, such as *'a'cum (ovdei, kochavim umzzilot*, "workers/worshippers/slaves of the stars and constellations"), changing this to *goyyim*, "nations." Maimonides preferred the more ambiguous title of *De'ah* (vs. *Ma'dah*) for "knowledge." Even in this new translation, Strauss gives examples of mistranslations: for *ben Adam* (literally "son of Adam," is translated as "man"), the translator used four different translations—"majority of mankind," "men," "the people," and "children of men." There is ambiguity in Maimonides' use of "son" (Guide, 1.7). I leave aside for now further details of this critique.

But there is an elegant example of the profound significance of context to understand Maimonides. In the *Book of Knowledge*, and more significantly perhaps in the *Guide*, Maimonides begins each chapter with this phrase from *Genesis* 21:33:

"בשמ יהוה אל עולמ"

"*B'shem Yehovah, El Olam*," "In the name of Yehovah, God of the Universe"

What's the context? *This* Abraham calls out after he digs his first wells in Beersheba and gives seven ewes to Avimelech to secure these wells (his legacy to Isaac). *This* Abraham calls out after dissimulating to Avimelech that Sarah was Abraham's sister (to prevent being killed by Avimelech to possess Sarah).[13] *This* Abraham calls out just after Abraham has desert-exiled his wife Hagar and her son, Ishmael, at both Sarah's demand and God's command. Finally, *this* Abraham wails just before the *Akeda*, when *this* God tests Abraham's faith by commanding him to sacrifice his son Isaac to God.

That is, the almost formulaic "*B'shem Yehovah, El Olam*," is embedded in a series of terribly powerful moments: the near-betrayal of his wife (and Avimelech), the ownership of his first properties (wells in this desert), Abraham's abandonment (at the edge of desert-death) of his concubine and first son, Ishmael, and the near-sacrifice of Isaac, *not* his only son. For the student of the Torah, for the believer, "in the name of Yehovah," is not a neutral, albeit anodyne phrase.

Later, in his writings, Maimonides cites *Job* as a late proclamation against a transactional view of God; serve Him out of love/awe only. The *Akeda* may be a model for *Job*.[14] At least, for Jews.

If we take Maimonides at his word (and let us do that for now in order to understand him), then beginning each chapter of the *Guide* with "*B'shem Adonai, El Olam*," is not simply formulaic, some magical incantation. Rather, it reminds us of the gravity of the moment of Abraham's life (and of the beginning of Judaism and its relationship to God); he reminds us of *the gravity of what we will study in this chapter*, the seriousness of our study.

We close with Maimonides' audience for the *Mishnah Torah*. It is for everyone (adults), from the simplest to the most educated. However, even as early as in this text, Maimonides shows that he understands the value in writing with ambiguity, with multiple meanings (not just "two" as implied by the preface "ambi." It *is* "ambi" if we consider there are two meanings, "overt" and "covert"). The majority should be able to read the text and understand the Laws. But for those with greater knowledge, more questions, and those influenced by the science of the surrounding culture (specifically those who have studied Aristotle), the text should contain layers of meaning that will help them, without jeopardizing the faith or understanding of the majority. We will learn in the next chapter how Maimonides carries the art of ambiguity, simultaneous hiding and revealing, to a higher level, even as he overly states that this text מורה נבוכים, *Moreh Nevuchim, The Guide of the Perplexed,* was "written" as letters to one student, one pupil well-educated in *Torah* and the sciences. One student who is left with the dangerous double dilemma of perplexity: question science *or* question Judaism.

As we turn to studying *The Guide* in the next chapter, we note historically that the Jews appeared to have at least two reactions to their exile, their loss of *terra firma,* their loss of footing, their loss of the Land of Israel, and the sense of physical community it provided:

One reaction, summarized above, religious scholars recognized that one must codify the Jewish Laws *in writing,* despite the stipulation that certain things *should not be written.* Writing preserves the otherwise wandering nature of purely oral transmission.

The second reaction was a deep plunge into mysticism (Scholem, 2013). Hebrew letters also represent numbers. Hebrew mystical texts arose around the Christ/Roman era about how the meaning of certain letters, the sum of a word's letters, for instance, had mystical meaning. If one could decipher these numerical chimeras, one could elevate one's soul. But, in this belief system, it is treacherous to move up the levels of elevation, for instance, through seven levels, where angels safeguard the gates of entry.

We will see how Maimonides had his own version of a form of mystical thinking, but one that rejected any magical formulae. To jump to the second part of this book, Freud dismantles in his first chapter the multiple "mystical," purely symbolic schools of dream interpretation. So too, Maimonides. But, we will learn, he believed and tried to demonstrate that if one studied God's creations carefully, if one tried to grasp some nature of God— incorporeal, unified, timeless—[15] one elevates one's soul to understand something that words can lead us up to, but is beyond the expression of words. Again, we remind the reader of dreams: they "occur" mostly visually; they are transmitted to ourselves and our listeners with words, a transformation that may not always capture the full experience of the vision. But, even these visual representations in the original dream come from some pre-visual substrate, some thoughts/feelings/wishes, which precede the visual and possibly the verbal. Just as "awe" may be inexpressible in words.

Notes

1 For a summary of the historical development of Mishnah, Gemarrah, and Babylonian/Jerusalem Talmuds, see the 1911 EB article (https://en.wikisource. org/wiki/1911_Encyclopædia_Britannica/Talmud). While there are more up-to-date accounts, including Halbertal's, the 1911 touches on major dates and developments.

2 To justify which commentaries on the Laws are most valid, Maimonides uses an almost "democratic" criterion: the commentaries accepted by the overall Jewish communities dispersed widely in exile are those that are more valid. Local rabbis' opinions are, well, opinions.

Relying on a kind of popular vote for accepted validity appears at odds with Maimonides' *Guide* written for the (spiritually/intellectually) elite. And yet, this tension between the *hoi palloi* and the elite is inherent in much of Maimonides' ideas about even *Torah*, let alone his works. Language's ambiguity permits one to speak and write to a greater audience and the listeners' inner filters will hear what is understood at their own level. This reminds us of the four sons at Passover: one should answer the questions of the four sons according to their level of (and desire for) comprehension, from the wise to the simple, who cannot even formulate the question.

3 The word "*Halachah*" has ambiguity embedded. It is intended to mean the Laws by which to live a Jewish life. But it shares a root with *holech*, to walk. Hence, *Halacha* is more literally how to "walk the proper path of life." As Biblical Hebrew tends to be more bodily-centered and more concrete (Alter, 2019), we are inclined to read *Halachah* in both meanings, *but* "to walk the walk" is more important than prayers or even fragrant burnt offerings. (Isaiah I:11–17: "Why need I all your sacrifices?.... You shall no longer bring false grain offering, it is incense of abomination to me.... Wash, become pure,/ Remove your evil acts from My eyes./ Cease doing evil./ Learn to do good,/ seek justice. /Make the oppressed happy,/ defend the orphan,/ argue the widow's case" (Alter, 2019).)

4 A too brief historical overview of these commentaries preceding Maimonides and their historical vicissitudes is as follows: The Persians conquered the Babylonians in the sixth century BCE, permitting Jews to return to Israel. In the fourth century, Alexander and the Greeks conquered the Persians. Thus, there were two centers of Jewish studies—Israel, under the Greeks, the Hashmonaim, and Rome, and Babylonia, under the Persian Zoroastrian regime. The Mishnah was an attempt by Yehuda HaNassi to pick the essential pronouncements of the *Tana'im* (scholars from the period of Ezra and Nehemiah until the destruction of the Temple but largely from the period of the Hashmonain state) that one needed to observe the *mitzvoth*. These pronouncements are called *mishna'ot*. Pronouncements that were not selected are referred to as *Bri'tot* in the *Talmud*.

The *Mishnah was edited by HaNassi* after the Roman conquest (70 CE.) Its many volumes contain the *mishna'ot* ordered into "tractates" which are then organized into six "orders." The *Talmud* is composed of the *Mishnaot* and the discussions of them by the Amora'im (who came after the *Tana'im*). These discussions are called the Gemora. Together, Mishnah and Gemorah constitute the *Talmud*. The Talmudic debates occur after the codification of the *Mishna'ot* (E. Salzburg, personal communication, 2022).

5 Translating "awe" is problematic. The contemporary Hebrew words for "awe" overlap with "fear": יְרַאת כָּבוֹד *(yirat kavod)* or 'respectful fear'; יִרְאָה, *yirah*, "fear"; מוֹרָא, "*moraa*" (the reader will "hear" the latter's homonym for "teacher," but spelled with a silent ה at the end). We suggest the Hebrew, (בהלמ) *b'helem*, which is more like shock or amazement, although to our knowledge, Rambam does not use *b'helem*.

6 *Nicomachean Ethics* I.13, the human's *rational principle* (Greek: λόγον ἔχον) (rationally organized efforts), is added to the *nutritive* life of plants and the *instinctual* life of animals. *Deliberative imagination* defines man (*De anima* III.11).

7 I thank Yikun Wu, Ph.D., *eshet chayil*, for this insight.
8 For this and the following on Judeo-Arabic, I thank Prof. Daniel Birnstiel, Goethe-Universität Frankfurt am Main | FB09-Institut für Islamstudien, and for the Hebrew translation, my dear friend Myron Joshua.
9 It is a feeling which he would like to call a sensation of "'eternity," a **feeling as of something limitless, unbounded—as it were "oceanic."**

> • One may, he thinks, rightly call oneself religious on the ground of this **oceanic feeling** alone, even if one rejects every belief and every illusion.
> • I cannot discover this '**oceanic' feeling** in myself. It is not easy to deal scientifically with feelings (Freud, 1930).

10 *Tradutorre, Traditore*, Walter Benjamin reminded us: "translator is traitor" (Szajnberg, 2023).
11 This recalls Freud's idea of reversal in dream work, which we cover in Part II.
12 Now available online "harambam.org."
13 When God reveals to Avimelech this ruse, the king doesn't "take" Sarah sexually and complains to Abraham how he had jeopardized him and his people. Avimelech acts—rather *doesn't* act—in contrast to the much later David.
14 See Josef Stern for an understanding of Maimonides' interpretation of the *Akeda, which emphasizes the verses after 1–10 as an affirmation of life. May 5, 2010, University of Chicago, Franke Forum.* https://www.youtube.com/watch?v=ky3i-fL4Vmwo (Stern, 2010).
15 We ask the reader's indulgence if we suggest that these characteristics describe man's Unconscious, at least its "timelessness" and its sense that it is incorporeal.

References

Alter, R. (2019). *The Hebrew Bible*. Norton
Freud, S. (1929). Letter from Sigmund Freud to Romain Rolland, July 14, 1929. *Letters of Sigmund Freud 1873–1939*, 51:388.
Freud, S. (1930). Civilization and Its Discontents. *The Standard Edition of the Complete Psychological Works of Sigmund Freud*, 21:57–146.
Green, A. (2019). "Fear and Awe in Maimonides." https://repository.yu.edu/bitstream/handle/20.500.12202/6915/Alex%20Green-%20Fear%20Awe%20Maimonides%20Bonhoeffer%2041-57%202019.pdf?sequence=1&isAllowed=y
Halbertal, M. (2014) Maimonides. Princeton U. Press.
Josephus (1984). The Jewish War. Penguin.
JPS TANAKH, Jewish Publication Society, 1999. JPS Philadelphia.
Klein, Y. (1968). Lecture for NCD on Aristotle's Man. University of Chicago.
Lerner, R. (2000). Maimonides' Empire of Light: Popular Enlightenment in an Age of Belief, p. 144. University of Chicago Press.
Maimonides (2019). On the Regimen of Health. Trans. Gerrit Bos. Brill Academic Publishers
Maimonides Mishneh Torah, Translated by Hyamson (1937). On Sefaria: https://www.sefaria.org/texts/Halakhah/Mishneh%20Torah
Mendelsohn, D. (2020). Three Rings. U of Virginia Press.
Scholem, G. (2013). *Origins of the Kabbalah*. Trans. Zwi Werblowsky. Princeton University Press.
Stern, J. (2010). The Unbinding of Isaac. University of Chicago, Franke Forum.

Stern, J. (2013). The Matter and Form of Maimonides' Guide. Harvard.

Strauss, L. (1963). Introduction: Maimonides' Guide of the Perplexed. Translated by Shlomo Pines. U of Chicago Press.

Strauss, L. (2013). The Literary Character of *The Guide of the Perplexed*. In *Leo Strauss on Maimonides: The Complete Writings*. University of Chicago.

Szajnberg, N. (Spring 2023). Psychic Mimesis: From Bible to Homer, to Now. Lexington.

TANAKH, Jewish Publication Society, 1999. JPS Philadelphia.

Winnicott, D. (1974). The Maturational Processess and the Facilitating Environment. IUP.

Chapter 4

Guide

Maimonides, that wandering refugee exile, would have known well by heart, *in his heart*, King David's psalm of exile and homecoming:

> "When Israel came out of Egypt; House of Jacob/
> The sea saw and fled/
> The Jordan turned its back/
> The mountains danced like rams,
> Hills like lambs of the flock....
> Before the Master, Whirl, O earth,
> Before the God of Jacob,
> Who turns the rock into a pond of waters
> Flint to a spring of water."
> Psalms, 114, King David (transl., Alter, 2019)

בְּצֵאת יִשְׂרָאֵל, מִמִּצְרָיִם; בֵּית יַעֲקֹב
הים ראה וינס
הירדן יסב לאחור
ההרים רקדו כאילים
גבעות כבני צאן

. . .

מלפני אדוני חולי ארץ
מלפני אלוהי יעקב
ההפכי הצור אגם מים
הלמיש למעינו מים.

I begin with Strauss's interpretation of David's psalm: when Israel is liberated from slavery, when it finds its belief in this one, eternal, incorporeal God, when Israel's feet land on its homeland, *then* their world transforms from dormant to beauty, from lifeless to lively, from inert stones to dancing and graceful rams, from old to young. All are "spontaneously" transformed, a spontaneity when Israel roots itself in its land, when the soul is united with the body. So, Strauss suggests (1963), Maimonides transforms the *Torah* to unveil its hidden beauty, the elegance beneath the overt 613 Laws of Jewish life. So too, Strauss transforms the bramble of Maimonides' *Guide* into a garden of our delight. We will rely on Halbertal, Josef Stern, and Strauss

DOI: 10.4324/9781003358213-4

to clarify the paths through this otherwise maze of difficulties; they will be Arachne's thread so that we are not lost in Maimonides' purposefully constructed labyrinth, and we will not be consumed by the confused perplexity represented by the half man, half beast Minotaur.

The only aim of this chapter, fitting with this book, *is to learn what Maimonides discovers about the mind's mechanisms and how he uses them to conceal and reveal secrets. Maimonides discoveries of mechanisms of inner life,* we will see later in this book, are consistent, even foretell, Freud's discoveries of the work of dream life. We will not in this book attempt to teach nor explain Maimonides' *Guide*: as Leo Strauss wrote, this takes years of dedicated reading preferably with a guide. We refer the interested reader to Strauss, Halbertal, Stern, and, of course, Maimonides for this greater endeavor.

For our more modest effort—revealing Maimonides' mechanisms of mind—I begin with Strauss, as he early on recognized the literary genre of exoteric/esoteric within which Maimonides' two major lifeworks—the youthful *Mishnah Torah* and the more mature *Guide for the Perplexed*—are nestled. Strauss's writings on Maimonides weigh in at over 600 pages, from 1930 through 1968. Of these, we select three works that concentrate on the *Guide*: "The Literary Character of the Guide" (1941); "Introduction to Maimonides *Guide of the Perplexed*" (1960); and "How to Begin to *Study Guide of the Perplexed*" (1963). The first paper is the sapling of his ideas; the second and third are ring accretions which strengthen and develop the towering Redwoods of his ideas and how they branch out, offering a sheltering canopy, to a greater understanding.

Afterward, we will turn to Halbertal's and Josef Stern's illuminating studies of the *Guide*. Along the way, we will draw parallels to Freud's model of dream work and interpretation, to our chthonic inner life.

Maimonides famously initiates the reader's challenge and dilemma.

On the one hand, he says he will deal with only two matters in this Guide: *Ha Ma'aseh Bereshit* and *Ha Ma'aseh Merkavah*: the story/matter/journey of the Beginning *(Bereshit)* and the story/matter/journey of the Chariot *(Merkavah)*. These are two of the greater secrets of the *Torah*. Then, he adds that *Bereshit* is a study of physics (in Aristotelian terms) and *Merkavah* is a study of metaphysics (the heavenly beings and the Divine).

But, he then states clearly, bluntly, that this book will *not* be about physics nor about metaphysics.

Another paradox. He states openly that the *Talmud* prohibits teaching about its secrets.[1] Or, one can do so only in speech. And only to one student at a time. And even so, one can teach only the chapter headings *(rashei perakim)* of the secrets. And the reader will hear that the phrase *rashei perakim* also refers to the opening phrases of each week's *Torah* portion.

Maimonides demurs, begs our understanding. Because of the extended exile of Jews and the wide dispersion (at least from Yemen to Spain, Europe to North Africa), there is a danger of losing oral-aural transmission of knowledge. So, he will write down what he has learned on his own, but in a cryptic manner with the dispersal of the chapter headings. And he will give us, the knowledgable reader, the details of *how* he has hidden the secret meanings in *Torah*. And, it is *Torah* to which he returns (as in the term *Mishnah*).

Anyhow, he explains, he is not writing a book, a s*efer*, but an *agadah*, a storytelling or narrative, much in the tradition of the oral *Torah* (or epic poems).

By the way, the two great secrets of *Torah* about which he will write are only two and the greatest ones: *Bereshit* and *Merkavah*. But the great secret of the Torah, we remind the reader, is the meaning of the tetragrammaton of God's name, *Yehovah*. Of this Maimonides will not write. This he omits. But, he will tell us below that one of his techniques for hiding secret meanings is "omission." So, is he revealing the tetragrammaton meaning in some manner also, using his technique of omission?

And Maimonides then states that his concern in the *Guide* is to reconcile Torah with reason (Strauss, 2013, p. 418).

Maimonides clarifies further what this *Guide* is not: it is *not* a book of philosophy because "to be a Jew and a philosopher is mutually exclusive" (Strauss, 1960). And it is *not* a book of theology, which is not a Jewish term (certainly not in Jewish medieval times) (Strauss, 1960, p. 434 ff).[2] Intriguingly, just as Maimonides begins the *Guide* by clarifying that *God is defined by what he is not* (not corporeal, not fragmented, not temporally defined), he begins it by helping us see what the *Guide* is not, and he defines its boundaries. Like Michelangelo's chiaroscuro shading, Maimonides uses the "what is not" to help reveal what is.

Even in his Introduction, Maimonides cleverly uses two techniques—misdirection and concealment—to "reveal" to us how the *Guide*, like *Torah*, will unveil its truths. Maimonides cites Proverbs 25, verse 11 to "explain" how he will write this work:

'תפוחי זהב במשכיוות כסף/דבר דבר על אפניו'

"Golden apples (with)in ornamental silver/words spoken before his face"

Stern (2018) argues in detail that Maimonides means to indicate to the reader that words have ambiguous meanings that both the Torah and the Guide use. Like our looking through a silver filigreed bowl, we see hints of the golden apples it embraces.

But, like some prestidigitation, Maimonides misdirects us from a clearer statement about *Guide*/*Torah*'s style with words. Misdirects us from what is "hidden" in plain sight, in the same Proverb 25, but earlier, verse 2-4; he "omits", in our judgment, the clearer statement:

כבד אלהים הסתר דבר דבר/וכבד מלכים חקר דבר:/שמים לרום וארץ לעמק/ולב מלכים אין חקר:/הגו סיגים מכסף/ויצא לצרף כלי.

"God's honor is to hide a matter,/The honor of kings to probe a matter./

The heavens for height, and the earth for depth/
But the heart of kings is beyond probing.
Remove the dross from sliver,
And for the refiner) metalsmith[3]), the vessel comes out"

(transl., Alter, 2019)

Here, per King Solomon, God's aim is to hide the "word/thing" and those of us kingly enough will try to dig deep to find the "word/thing," which in turn is a precious metal that has been extracted from dross. Maimonides "directs" us to the more allusive, we suggest, verse 11 about golden apples in a silver ornamental bowl, but Maimonides also is misdirecting us from the earlier verse that says more straightforwardly that the precious word/thing, דבר, *(davar)* is God's hidden treasure and we can dig deep to discover and then refine the precious metal from the dross. Maimonides will not only tell us what he will do, but he shows us.

Strauss in his 1963 "Begin to Study[4]" opens with an outline of the entire book, which we will articulate below.

Yet, as we read, we understand that Maimonides' *Guide* has several trajectories. It begins with the visual, the imagined. What can be more visual than imagining the creation of our world, from *tohu v'vohu*, void and emptiness, to light and dark, to sky and water, to separation of waters above and below, to separation of ocean waters from land, to populating the sky and the waters, to the land filled with creatures above and below, and finally to creating "man" in God's "likeness," in his "image"? This is a cacophony of visualization of the physical, a tour through natural sciences. In Maimonides' term, it is the sublunar universe, about which Maimonides believed Aristotle was accurate.

Then we have the hallucinatory chariot chapter of Ezekiel. This is the supra-lunar universe, the dwelling of God and the angels, the eternal beings. And this also is a highly visual, highly imaginative scenario. It is spectacular, and it is a *spectacle* in the sense of Aristotle's term in his *Poetics*[5]: while a lower form of art, in Aristotle's view, it captures and captivates us. As do dreams ... an art felt as if emerging from our lower forms. An art form, the dream, that Freud was able to transform via words into words to make sense of our lower forms.

In his opening Psalm from David, Maimonides quotes:

הִנֵּי מקום איתי ניצותתה אל הצוה. והיה בעבור'

"Here, is a place[6] by me and you (Moses) will stand poised[7] on the rock. And (my) "isness"[8] passes over..."

(Alter, 2019; Exodus 33: 21–22)

This returns us to Strauss's opening quote. God has Moses stand on an inert rock. Moses is standing poised (that is, as prepared for action), enlivened, by God's presence passing over him. Moses is differentiated from the inert stone by God's presence. This reminds us of Michelangelo's unfinished sculpture of the two slaves in the Louvre basement, one struggling to emerge from the inert stone from which he is carved.[9]

Maimonides insists that each word in the *Guide* is carefully selected, and purposeful he cautions us that to understand the *Guide* (and the *sitrei torah*, the secrets/contradictions of *Torah*), we need to pay careful attention to the words and the sentences.

Well, let's begin at the beginning: The title. The Hebrew title is *Moreh Nevuchim*, from Maimonides' Arabic title *Dalalat al-ha'irin*. The Hebrew title was translated by ibn Tibbon, who sent all his translations to Maimonides for review and approval. So, for the moment, let's assume that the Hebrew title is "accurate" and captures Maimonides' Arabic title.

In fact, Maimonides states in the introduction to this book that he chose the (Arabic) title because the book's objective was to explain the terms and parables that cause "great perplexity" *(hayrah shadydah)* even to one who is "perfect in religion and character and has studied philosophy" (Gesundheit and Hadad, in Stern 2013).

Both words in the title give us great room for consideration. The simple *moreh* generally is translated as Hebrew for the (male) teacher. *Torah* is usually quickly understood as the five books of Moses. But literally and simply it is translated as (female) "teaching." That is, ibn Tibbon (with Maimonides' approval) has connected this "Guide" by titling it *Moreh* with its feminine counterpart, the *Torah*. The male *Moreh* embraces the female *Torah*. In this sense, the *Guide* is a more sophisticated version, a **return to** the *Mishnah Torah*, as it is a **return** to *Torah*.[10]

*Nevuchim i*s a unique term in *Torah*. Maimonides refers to a passage in the *Torah* in which other nations, such as the Egyptians, believe that the Israelites have wandered for 40 years (in a relatively small area near *Qadesh Barnea*) because they were "perplexed," uncertain of their direction or navigation. But, Maimonides argues, following the rabbis, that in fact there *was* a direction deemed by God (via Moses) for this generation of wandering Israelites. At least one reason was that the enslaved Israelites were not prepared to face the battles to regain their land. Recall the passages (Alter, 2019, Numbers 13: 1–33; Deuteronomy 1: 22–40) in which Moses sends 12 princes from each tribe to spy out the land; ten return fearful of entering this land, saying that the inhabitants appear like giants (ילדי הענק, *yaldei ha'anak*, "children of giants" (Alter, 2019, Numbers 13:28).[11] Moses wisely concludes that the Israelites are not prepared to enter and battle for their freedom. While the Israelites were politically free, they remained enslaved in their minds (Fromm, 1941). The Israelites wandered for 40 years so that both the previous generation of slaves would die out and a new generation born in the desert, hardened, hungry to find a true homeland would be prepared to battle and build one. That is, Maimonides' title suggests (or hints) that the perplexed can be transformed from the one hungering, yet confused and fearful to inhabit a homeland, to one who can engage in the struggle to become rooted and feel at home. This *Guide* can assist, but only with proper persistence, intellectual courage, and desire. Then, this *Moreh* will help lead them into a new home for a freer spirit.

Now, Maimonides cautions us that each word of his *Guide* is carefully selected. Furthermore, to understand a word, one needs to examine how it is embedded and its context. Again, he confounds us when he advises his translator, ibn TIbbon, that translation should be exquisitely accurate to the word, yet the translator should be creative in transmitting the heft of the ideas. Pines, in his private correspondence with Strauss—they had been colleagues and friends for decades from their German era—complained that Strauss was being too demanding about exact translation, when Pines would tend toward interpretative translation (Kraemer and Stern, 1999). Benjamin—who translated professionally, earned his keep at times as a translator—cautioned us that *traditure traditorre*, "the translator is traitor." He could have been cautioning the reader of translation, and/or he could have been cautioning us that this translator (such as himself) may be traitorous for creative purposes. To which of the contradictory Maimonides should we listen when we try to read his *Guide* in another language: the demanding word accuracy or the "creative" translations? For the sake of our reading, we choose to follow Strauss and sail close to the winds of accuracy, recognizing that with translating headwinds, we may need to tack port and starboard to achieve our home port of understanding.

So, we now turn to two more central words for Maimonides, *bereshit* and *merkavah*, מרכבה, בראשית, the "beginning" and "chariot."

The Hebrew בראשית contains the three-letter root, ראש "head." That is, the beginning of the world, begins with the "head." This makes sense. Whereas the "word" (דבר) of God creates thing (דבר) (sky, waters, earth, living things), in the beginning, בראשית, in the very first word of *torah*, these come from the ראש, the "head."[12] We in a sense have two initiating points in the *Guide*: the visual (creation of things including the universe) *and* something from the "head." Maimonides later defines two major features of our minds, our heads, in Bible: imagination and intellect. The imagination, he later clarifies, is a feature, a talent of prophets in order to translate or transmit to people what he with his intellect understands from God. The intellect is the highest form of achievement, one which mankind can use to approach asymptotically what is an essence of God. At the beginning of the *Guide*, hence, we start with both visual and head.

Now to the second topic, secret, of the *Guide*, מרכבה, *merkavah*, "chariot." The root of מרכווה is רכב, or 'wagon' (today, it is used to describe a car or vehicle). The infinitive of this is, להרכיב, *l'harkiv*, to assemble. Today, a train is called רַכֶּבֶת, *rakevet*, that is something "assembled," as trains are from individual cars.

And there is much to "assemble" in this chariot dream.

Let's look at some chapters from this "strangest of all prophets" (Alter, 2019, p. 1049) Ezekiel, (ca. 622–570 BCE) living in exiled Babylon and harnessing his dream to his predecessor, Isaiah (ca. 730 BCE in the land of Israel).[13]

Start with Isaiah, who sees more of the Lord than did Moses, who saw only His back. Isaiah says:

"....I saw the Master seated on a high and lofty throne, and the skirts of his robe ... Seraphim were stationed over him, six wings for each.../
...one of the seraphim flew down to me, in his hand a glowing coal in tongs that he had taken from the altar. And he touched my mouth and said,
'Look, this has touched your lips,/
And your crime is gone, your offense shall be atoned.'
And he (the Master) said, 'Go and say to this people:
...you must hear but you will not understand/
...you must see but you will not know.'"

(Isaiah 6: 1-10; Alter, 2019)

We "hear" not only the visual (transformed into words) but also the words of the Master (centuries later, borrowed by Christ).

Isaiah is the prototype for Ezekiel's two chariot ascents two centuries later, much more detailed, more elaborate, and scintillating. Listen to Ezekiel's words that transform his vision:

".a storm wind.a great cloud and fire flashing, and radiance all round it, and from within it like...amber from within fire. ...four living creatures and this was their look—-the likeness of a man being...each had four faces and four wings...Their legs were straight...and the soles of their feet like the sole of a calf's foot and they glittered like the look of burnished bronze. And there were human hands beneath their wings on their four sides...Their wings did not turn as they went; each went straight ahead. And the likeness of their faces—...a human...a lion on the right...and the face of bull to the left...and eagle to the four of them...each went straight ahead....The likeness of the creatures...was like burning coals of fire...had radiance and from the fire lightning came forth. ....One wheel was on the ground...the wheels ...were like chrysolite and a single likeness the faces of them had....a wheel is within a wheel. For their rims, they were high and they were fearsome and their rims were filled with eyes, all round....
...over the heads of the beasts —a platform like ...fearsome ice stretched over. And beneath the platform their wings....I heard the sound of their wings like the shout of many waters, like the sound of Shaddai...an uproar,...of an armed camp.

...above the platform...was like the look of sapphire stone—a throne, and above (it)...like a human form....the appearance of amber....from the look of his loins above and.below I saw like the look of fire....Like the look of the rainbow...the look of the likeness of the glory of the Lord. And I saw and fell on my face and heard a voice speaking."

We quote this significant portion since the *merkavah* is half of what Maimonides will explore in his *Guide*. And all of the above is the verbal transmission of a visual experience. Ezekiel does "hear" maybe even "feel" rushing winds, wings like many waters, and the sound of Shaddai, but this all precedes the words he will soon hear from his Master.

Again, we quote only a portion of Ezekiel's voice.

"And he said to me, 'Man, stand on your feet and I shall speak with you.' And a spirit entered me as He spoke. ...'Man, I send you to the Israelites, ... That have rebelled against Me....say to them, "Thus said the Master, the Lord....Listen to what I speak to you (Ezekiel). Open your mouth and eat what I give you." A hand was stretched out to me.... in it was the scroll of a book. And he unrolled it before me and it was written on both sides...dirges, lament and woe./

'...Eat this scroll and go speak to the house of Israel'.... And I ate and it became sweet as honey in my mouth."

(Ezekiel, Chapter 1–2; Alter, 2019)

Note, now Ezekiel *sees* God, *hears* Him, and even *tastes* the words God gives him. Ezekiel has ascended "higher," we might say, than either Moses or Isaiah: Isaiah eats a hot coal; Ezekiel, a scroll of honey. From this, in part, Maimonides develops an argument that it is possible to develop further (spiritually) even after the greatest of prophets, Moses. This, he suggests, is a model for us.

Aristotle argued that *mimesis* is imitation of nature, an act that differentiates man from animals. *Mimesis* is inherent in man and serves to evoke feelings (at least vicariously, even in the actor, if we follow Maimonides). Aristotle suggests that we learn through perceptual experiences to get closer to the "real" (Aristotle, *The Poetics*). We will see that for Maimonides, knowledge and *practice*, forms of mimesis (mimicry) of God's attributes — wisdom, intellect, compassion, justice, and so on—bring us asymptotically closer to God. This is a lifetime's effort.Intriguingly, for Maimonides, while "knowing" (the intellect) is a higher form of being, "doing" or practice (of the Laws) is central. In fact, we will learn later in his book, he sees "learning" as a form of doing, perhaps the highest form.[14] More specifically, Maimonides referred to his *Mishnah Torah* as "our greatest work," but his Guide as "my treatise" (or compilation, "*chibur*" חיבור) (Strauss, 2013).[15] The

Mishnah Torah represented actions; the *Guide*, opinions. But—and here Maimonides guides us around full circle to resolve an apparently dichotomous contradiction—*the greatest "action" is studying Torah. Only then does action accord with speech (Strauss, 1943).*

Maimonides offers another way to reconcile paradoxical statements, such as his distinction of the book, *Sefer*, from *chibur*, treatise/compilation. If *Sefer* represents "actions" and the chibur his "opinions," how do we weigh the value of one against the other? To which, Maimonides responds by quoting Proverbs 22:7:

> "Hearken to sages' words,/
>   Apply heart to my opinions."

And to the ambiguity inherent in Biblical Hebrew, Maimonides quotes Deuteronomy, 7:21:

> "The words of the wise are few, their meanings many."

A technique to understand the *Guide* includes our hearkening to its words, but applying our hearts, listening to the many meanings of words.

Let's turn to the structure of the Guide, before we learn what Maimonides reveals as his techniques of concealment.

Seven sections, 38 subsections, and overall divided into two major components: "Views" and "Acts." This is the raw structure.

I. *"Views"* explore five topics on what one "sees" in Torah:

1 God terms
2 God's existence, unity, and incorporeality
3 Prophets' endowment and training (translating ideas to visions for the people)
4 The chariot
5 Providence

II. *"Acts"* entail:

1 God's commandments
2 Man's perfection

Maimonides unites views and acts: *views endure if there are corresponding actions* (living out the commandments) (Strauss, 1963 p. 501).

Maimonides promises to explain *almost* all the commandments (3: 27-8), recognizing that a whole set of commandments, the *chukim*, are religiously *proscribed* from being explained: one should perform them without explanations (such as the prohibition against eating pork).

Then, he contradicts himself. He will explain only a *few* commandments (Strauss, p. 432). Which of the contradictions are we to believe? Maimonides offers us hints to answer this.

Maimonides sketches out three major techniques for secrecy before he details them: First, *each word* should be carefully examined, including its context.

Second, there are *deliberate contradictions* (playing with the ambiguity of the word *"histir"* which means both hidden and contradictory).

Third, he will *scatter the chapter headings (roshei perakim)*, again playing ambiguously with the literal meaning—"headings of his chapters"—and the allusion to the more familiar chapter headings of the *Torah.*

Until now, we have Maimonides' *goals* for the Guide and an outline of its *content*:

> To study two secrets of Torah:
> The creation and the chariot.
> To reconcile Torah and reason.

He will explain *Torah's words* and *parables* (Strauss, 1963; Halbertal, 2013; Stern, 2013)

He does this for us: to resolve our perplexities that otherwise could jeopardize our inner equilibrium and ennoblement.

By the way, about secrets, Maimonides points out that there are three meanings to a secret:

1 The *word* or parable can be a secret.
2 The *meaning* of a word/parable can be a secret.
3 The *thing* referred to can be a secret.

The Hebrew word דבר, "dvr" carries this ambiguity, meaning both "word" and "thing" as mentioned above.[16] Word ambiguity in Hebrew fosters ambiguity, even secrecy.

And we have Maimonides' insistence about what the Guide will not do: neither teach physics (i.e., the creation) nor metaphysics (i.e., the chariot). And he will not engage in philosophy[17] nor theology. He states the "will"s and the "won't"s of this *Guide.*

But the centrality of this chapter and this book's aim is to compare Maimonides' thoughts about mental mechanisms with Freud's. That is, the techniques by which our mindss work to conceal and reveal almost simultaneously. Let's turn to Maimonides' revelation about his techniques of hiding, revealing, and hinting. We turn to study the layers beneath the overt, the manifest narratives. Here is how he prepares us to decipher—for it is a cipher, this *Guide* (or our minds)—this *agadah,* this telling.

The Techniques: Maimonides' Elements of Style

We can begin with an overall contradiction cited by Maimonides. The Law says that it is illegal to teach the secrets. The secrets are impossible to convey, because we are corporeal beings, of the flesh. This is in itself contradictory or at least inconsistent, Strauss argues (1963): if it is impossible to teach the secrecy, then why prohibit its teaching?

Maimonides gives some general principles. Truths should flash up, then disappear. The *Torah's* style (for concealing/revealing) is to use parable to hide enigmas. But the *Guide's* style is to be obscure and brief. Use three types of "irregularities" (Strauss, 1960):

1   Disruptions of narrative. For instance, in *Torah*, the lengthy Joseph story is "interrupted" by the Tamar/Judah near-incestuous union. Or in the *Guide*, the chapters on God's "body" or emotional features (his arm, his finger, his wrath) is suddenly interrupted by chapters on "man." These interruptions are intended to convey hidden meanings.
2   To begin a chapter, the use of an Arabic article prior to a Hebrew noun at times; other chapters being with Hebrew articles with Hebrew nouns. These irregularities point to differences in meaning (p. 461 ff).
3   Use intentional perplexities such as variations on a theme. For instance, in the *Job* story, his four "friends" all give the same argument for why Job should reject God. But, as we read closely, the fourth interlocutor plays variations on this theme. The variations hint at something meaningful. Freud, we will demonstrate in the second part of this book, makes much of variations on a dream report when it is repeated. A second example of variations is Isaiah's vision of God compared to the two Ezekiel visions.

But the guiding principle of the genus of the *Guide* is to use contradictions. Maimonides uses six types of contradictions and gives hints as to how to discover the truth within the contradictions:

1   State contradictions separated by a few pages.
2   State contradictions in passing.
3   Imply contradictions. For example, to state that the *Guide* will teach about the chariot; that the chariot equals metaphysics; and that the *Guide* will *not* teach metaphysics.
4   Repeat a statement, but with either *additions* or *omissions* that change the meaning of the original statement. An example is Maimonides quoting from Aristotle on "touch," but leaving out two final words that would change the meaning of Aristotle's true view (Strauss, 1964).
5   Embed internal contradictions.

6 Ambiguity. Specifically, there should be an "external" meaning versus an "internal" meaning which are ambiguously contending. For
instance, one meaning—an *external*, obvious one—is for the sake
of *society's well-being*. A more *internal*, hidden meaning leads to
"truth," *for the enlightened* student. Maimonides cites the Biblical
phrase, "A word fitly spoken," and interprets this to mean that a fitly
spoken word has two faces: one facing society; the other facing inner
perplexity.

Maimonides continues by hinting to us how to sort out the wheat from the
chaff of contradictions.

Secrecy is equivalent to rarity. The truth will be found in the more rare
statement. Maimonides' powerful example is the Biblical שמע ישראל, אדוני
אלוהינו, אדוני אחד '"*Sh'ma Yisrael, Adonai Eloheinu Aldonai Echod!*". This from
Deuteronomy is one of the few references to God's unity. Yet its truth is
central to Jewish belief.

Common words are important— such as "seemingly," "almost," and
"perhaps." These are tip-offs to some truth that will follow. Here is a stunning example that is also central to Freud's technique of dream interpretation, particularly used in his Irma dream, as we will detail in the second half
of this book.

Finally, Maimonides uses the Talmudic imperative that *if* one were to
teach the Torah's secrets, one must only teach the chapter headings *"rashei
perakim."* And as if to put guard rails around even this, Maimonides tells us
that he will sow these seeds, scatter them, throughout the *Guide*.[18]

These techniques are clear, simple, and terribly challenging to use.

And these techniques for concealing and revealing significant (esoteric)
meanings below also correct external manifest meanings that link us to
dream interpretation.

How so? Reading great literature, as Auerbach argued persuasively, is
reading the development of the inner life of mankind; culture is the distilla-
tion of the creativity of our minds. When Maimonides reads *Torah* so meticulously, he not only clarifies the multiple layers of meaning within a passage,
but he also teaches us something about the creative author of this text.
Whether this "author" is God, or a series of writers (men or a woman[19]),
matters not. For as Maimonides points out, God as the author of *Torah*
wrote it for the children of mankind בני אדם, "b'nei Adam" to understand.
Hence, God's words are tailored to humankind's mind. Hence, by reading
meticulously, we also learn about the richness, even the potential richness of
humankind's inner life. So too of reading Maimonides: If we follow the
guidance of Strauss or Halbertal or Stern, we will understand more clearly
Maimonides' writing, and Maimonides' mind, and hence, strengthen our
own inner lives.

The reader hears the bridge to Freud. For, as we will explore the better known story of Freud and dreams in the second part of this book, learning about how to understand the layers of meanings of dreams teaches us about the richness of our inner lives. It teaches us how we both conceal and (ambivalently) reveal our deeper inner lives. But we will reveal ourselves (even to ourselves) only if we are trained, if we are worthy to learn our own secrets.

Notes

1　The word "*histir*," in Hebrew, is translated as "secret," but also means "contradiction" in Biblical Hebrew (Strauss, 1963). Maimonides uses "contradiction" as a major concealing/revealing technique.

2　For more detailed explanations of why Maimonides is not "philosophy" nor "theology" at least in the medieval terms he would have used, see Strauss (1960, 1963). We are not arguing that *today*, Maimonides might be read philosophically, as Halbertal does well.

3　I suggest this word, *Tsoref*, can be translated as goldsmith or metalsmith (Alter says, "refiner"), which ties it to verse 11, the filagreed or ornamented bowl and golden apples.

4　This is the Introduction to the Pines' book, while Strauss's 1960 essay is called, confusingly, "Introduction."

5　Spectacle is one of tragedy's six components: plot, character, diction, thought, spectacle, and lyric poetry.

6　"Place" is *maqom in Hebrew*. In post-Biblical Hebrew, *maqom* was also a term used to refer to God. But Maimonides keeps reminding us that he will write only about Torah, not post-Biblical matters. Or so he says, even as he alludes to *Talmud.*

7　Here, I follow Strauss and more recently Alter's (2019) meticulous translation of *nitzav*. This is one of the three Hebrew Biblical words that refer to standing (in addition to *amad ("stand")* and *qam (standing up or arising)*. As you will see, each of the three has different aspects of motion: *amad* is more static; *qam* is movement upward; and *nitzav* is an internal sense of being prepared to act. Here, in God's passing presence, Moses is prepared to act, differentiated from the static rock upon which he stands.

8　והיה is translated as "My Glory," per Strauss, p. 450.

9　The second slave appears deflated, either resigned to his enslavement, or, more hopefully, prior to his awakening in the sculptor's hands.

10　Strauss gives a short "course" on the richness of the root of *Moreh* and *Torah*, which is y-r-h ירה (p. 464). "It covers a range of words ... summarized as "to point," "to shoot" (an arrow), "to throw" (a stone), "to direct," "to teach," "to guide, "to instruct," and "to explain." He uses *A Hebrew and English Lexicon of the Old Testament, Based on William Genesis*, Trans. E. Robinson (Oxford: Clarendon, 1906/1953, pp. 434–436).

　　A passage in Exodus gives further richness to the root y-r-h. Here, the Israelites complain to Moses that the Sea of Maror is bitter, that they had better water in Egypt. God responds to Moses that he should throw a tree into the sea and it will sweeten the water. "ויורהו ה' עץ וישלך אל המים וימתקו המים." "And God threw a tree and sent it into the water and sweetened the water"

(Exodus, 15:25). This may also be connected to the concept of then Torah as the "tree of life," עץ חיים היה', "Etz Haiim Hih" (Personal communication from Myron Joshua).

11 Only two spies differ and believe that the land can be conquered, Joshua, who inherits Moses' mantle, and Caleb.

12 Of God, we may presume, but much of Maimonides' first part of the Guide argues that we should not think concretely of God's bodily features, but rather of metaphorical aspects of his being.

13 We will concentrate on the first 39 verses of Isaiah. There is scholarly consensus that the prophecy was written by at least three different writers, added to over a period of some two centuries, ranging from living in Israel, to the Babylonian conquest, and to prophecy prior to Ezra and Nehemiah's return to rebuild the temple and people (Alter, op. cit. p. 617 ff).
Verse 40 begins with Handel's recitative:

- Comfort ye my people
- Comfort ye
- Comfort ye my people
- Saith your God
- Saith your God. https://www.youtube.com/watch?v=H4yQJPHxBms

14 This reminds us of Arendt's distinction between *vita activa* and *vita contempletiva*. She argues that Galileo's invention of the telescope introduced the concept of not only thinking but also doing/making changes how we see the world. Yet, ironically, Arendt confesses that she felt more alive, more active in the course of thinking (Arendt, H. 1998. *The Human Condition* (second ed.). University of Chicago Press). We will see that Maimonides was of similar persuasion: learning and knowing are active "doing" processes that will guide how we act, or live out the Laws.

15 This is not strictly true, While Rambam did compare his Mishnah Torah and Guide as Sefer versus chibur, in his introductory words to his own Mishnah Torah, he wrote:
"וראיתי לחלק חיבור זה לארבעה עשר ספרים:, And I saw to apportion this **chibur** into fortune books." That is, he refers to his Mishnah Torah as both *chibur* and *Sefer*. Mishnah Torah introduction.

16 For example, we refer the reader to Jacob's admonishment of Joseph after his second "star-gazing" dream: that Jacob would שמר את הדבר', "Guard the thing" (Gen. 37:11).

17 For Maimonides, "philosophy" was divided into two major categories:

- Theoretical: mathematics, astronomy, etc...
- Practical: ethics, government. Strauss makes two points about "philosophy" as Maimonides understood it versus as we understand it today. For Maimonides philosophy meant Aristotelian or neo-Aristotelian (generally the Arabic philosophers) who study things from perceived beginnings of how things appear. Contemporary philosophy, per Strauss, is heavily influenced by Christian/European, particularly Germano-English (or French) thought (Strauss, 1963).

18 Interestingly, Maimonides' earlier work that summarizes his ideas is entitled שמונה פרקים *Shemoneh Perakim*, Eight Chapters.

19 Bloom H. and Rosenberg, J. (2004). *The Book of J.* Grove Press.

References

Alter, R. (2019). *The Bible and Writings*, Translation by R. Alter. Norton.

Fromm, E. (1941). *Escape from Freedom*. Holt.

Gesundheit, B. and Hadad, E. (2013). In: Josef Stern, *Maimonides, Matter and Form*. Harvard University Press.

Halbertal, M. (2014). *Maimonides*. Princeton.

Kraemer, J. and Stern, J. (1999). Shlomo Pines on the Translation of Maimonides Guide of the Perplexed. *Journal of Jewish Thought and Philosophy* 8 (1):13–24.

Maimonides. *The Guide of the Perplexed*. (1963). Trans. S. Pines. U of Chicago Press.

Maimonides, Mishneh Torah Transl. Hyamson (1937). Sefaria.

Stern, J. (2013). *Maimonides: Matter and Form*. Harvard.

Strauss, L. (1963). Introduction, *The Guide of the Perplexed*. Trans. S. Pines. U. of Chicago Press.

Strauss, L. (2013). *Leo Strauss, Writings on Maimonides*. University of Chicago Press.

Chapter 5

The Exoteric and Esoteric of Freud's Dream Book

"Truths flash up, then disappear," insists Maimonides. As can dreams. They flash up mostly visually, then can disappear, particularly as we try to recall the dreams in thought/words. If dreams possess certain "truths," how can we grasp these truths before they recede? This was Freud's challenge.

Dreams are the keystone for Freud's inner life inquiry (Freud, 1900; Erikson, 1954; Giovacchini, 2000; Lear 2005; Cohler, 2015). Freud's turn-of-the-millennium work introduced his model of mind: mental life is founded on the conflict between a wish and morality. Wishes that are consciously unacceptable are partially satisfied and revealed via dreams or symptoms. This implies:

1 The visual dream is the external face presented to the dreamer;
2 There is an internal "face" layered beneath that speaks to something truer to the dreamer, but *personally* unacceptable; and
3 There is an *internal drive* to reveal the concealed; a reverberating to know and not to know.

The dream book is divided into three sections:

Chapters 1–3 demonstrate that 1. dreams are wishes; 2. dreams don't foretell the future; and 3. formulaic "interpretations" are invalid.
Chapters 4–6 show the mechanisms used to disguise (and hence to unveil) the underlying meanings.
Chapter 7 is on the psychology of dream life.

The book was written backward. Chapter 7 was written first as the "Project for a Scientific Psychology" (Freud, 1895). The middle chapters came next. The first three chapters, including Freud's seminal "Irma" dream, came last. We are reminded of Saul Bellow's phrase, "Trouve avant de cherché," "Finding before seeking." From Charlie Citron's lips, but Humboldt's gift. (Bellow, 2008).

DOI: 10.4324/9781003358213-5

And, ironically, for a clearly written, tightly argued study, the dream book has *enigma engraved within*. Here's a significant enigma, which arises from Freud using his personal dreams as scientific demonstrations. Freud boldly states that for "Irma"—after he reports, then delicately dissects the dream and his associations—this is the most completely analyzed dream ever reported. And yet, Freud waits until Chapter 7, Section C, to state firmly that *no dream is completely analyzed until one connects with its infantile origins*. These are strikingly absent in the Irma chapter, omitted. One needs to hunt assiduously in his letters and other allusions to discover the infantile origins of this dream (Cohler, 2015).

And one can find infantile origins: buried in the footnote of the almost contemporaneous Screen Memory paper, the "Dream of the Botanical Monograph" (Freud, 1899), complemented by hints from Freud's contemporaneous correspondence with Fliess (1897–1899; Fliess, 1902). In a footnote to the screen memory, Botanical monographic dream, after Freud confesses that his favorite flower was the artichoke, he writes a thinly-disguised comment (Freud, 1899).[1] Two young boys and their two-year-old niece were playing in a dandelion field. The boys "molest" her in some manner. In Freud's self-analysis and revelations to Fliess, he adds his self-reproach over: sexual play with his younger sister Anna, guilt over the death of his half-brother when Freud was young, and hints of his nanny's aggressive sexual play with Freud. Amplifying the infantile is the more contemporary disastrous nose surgery by Fliess,[2] on a patient, Emma Ekstein, referred by and surgically assisted by Freud to solve her hysterical problems. *Now,* we have a more complete set of both infantile and day residue associations to the Irma dream. *Now* we have, as per Freud's criteria, the most complete analysis of the Irma dream.

And we have evidence of the degree to which the dream is associated, if not precipitated, by Freud's multiple self-reproaches and likely guilt over these childhood and adulthood associations. We complement this with Freud's father's death precipitating Freud's self-analysis and his discovery of the Oedipus complex in himself—parricide associated with incestuous mother desires—and the guilt associated with those feelings and we have a more complete understanding of what propelled Freud into his self-analysis and into writing this book of (self)-discovery. Cohler (op. cit.) among others have demonstrated *Freud's inner conflict* in writing this seminal dream book. (Grinstein, 1968; Anzieu, 1986; Grubrich-Simitis, 2000), Erikson (op. cit.), Giovacchini (2000)

Hence, we put Freud's dream book in the categories of *both exoteric and esoteric* writing. *Exo*terically, it outlines how to interpret the enigmatic manifest dream to get at the latent more meaningfully. *Eso*terically, Freud omits (and admits to this) some associations that are too revealing and possibly damaging to his reputation. *Eso*terically, this cardinal dream is closest to Freud's autobiography, much more so than his anodyne if factual *Selbstdarstellung* (Freud, 1925; Szajnberg, 1992).

Perhaps Freud is *un*aware that he misspeaks when he calls the Irma dream *completely* analyzed; he writes as if he hasn't stated clearly in Chapter 7 (the first chapter written) that infantile origins are needed for a full analysis. We need not speculate on whether this was a parapraxis or by conscious intent: for *esoteric* classification, we need only recognize that he leaves out fundamentally necessary meanings, as Strauss has taught us (Strauss, op. cit.; Szajnberg, 2023).

Our comments above establish the foundation to the intellectual architecture we will reconstruct with Freud's detailed plans on the inner structure of this home for Psyche and Eros, or at least the home for their dreams. We will progress through Freud's articulation of the need to conceal, followed by the three Unconscious concealing mechanisms—representation, displacement, condensation—used to conceal (and the fourth more conscious, secondary revision) and hence the techniques Freud discovered to guide us through the structure of our inner life. In doing so, we will draw parallels already mentioned in the first part of this book, to Maimonides' clarification of the exoteric and esoteric in *Torah*, the inner structures that Maimonides deeply honored as optimal for living a good life.

We will also see evidence of Maimonides' personal definition of parable (in *Torah* and *Guide*) as clarified by Stern, a mechanism that is different from exoteric/esoteric: parable tries to express (for Maimonides) the (verbally) inexpressible; to "say" some concepts that because we are of flesh, we cannot fully grasp or at least express. So, too, for Freud, we reach two limits of dream interpretation: the more conscious one is the limit of what we are able to express publicly (including ourselves) because it may harm our reputation; the second and more elusive limit is when we reach the navel of the dream, which, like mushrooms' mycelia, reach beneath the ground in a tangled mass of interwoven relationships that aren't expressible in words. In a later chapter, we will review the rich research on pre-verbal and pre-sentence development: how we have concepts and feelings that we can *show* without words in infancy, but may not be expressible in words. For instance, the one-year-old will *show* in almost narrative actions his or her attachment to a parent, before the words to say it. An 18-month-old will *show* (with pleasure, even excitement) that he or she gets it that another person has a separate mind that the child can influence, before having the words to say it (Stern, 1985; Szajnberg et al., 1989). Stern has suggested that we evolve four internal self-representations: the first three are pre-verbal; once the verbal self evolves, we can articulate more, but we distance ourselves from our early self-development (Stern, 1985; 2010).

We will see how Freud's mechanisms of concealment complement Maimonides: (conscious) concealing techniques. A corollary is that both Freud and Maimonides had access to preconscious and unconscious mental mechanisms of "defense" of concealing and revealing. We will learn, most of all, how Freud's ideas about how to reveal the hidden are similar to

Maimonides'. Finally, we will see how Maimonides and Freud had similar motivations for their researches: by studying the hidden in our most precious "texts" (*Torah*, psyche/dreams), we not only learn about hidden meanings, but also ennoble our lives. Both were, to some degree, concerned that superficial misunderstandings of their ideas could lead to societal censure; both were correct. This is not an intellectual or philosophical exercise for Maimonides or Freud; it is one of our most precious tasks to live a fuller, better life.

Our first task is to review the Irma dream and the lessons Freud derive from it. Then we will turn to the three mental defense mechanisms of dream work (distortion/revelation) and their "rules." Then we will draw parallels to the degree that they exist with Maimonides' techniques for concealing/ revealing as outlined in the first part of this book. Maimonides' primary concern is the betterment of mankind, including models for wisdom living (Adam, Abraham, Moses, God). Yet, he is aware that improving our inner lives is asymptotic and an ongoing effort. "Where id was, there ego shall be [*Wo Es war, soll Ich Werden*]. It is a work of culture, not unlike the draining of the Zuider Zee" (Freud, 1933, p. 80). That is, like the draining of the Netherlands seas, one must maintain the drained fertile lands with dykes and these must be periodically inspected, even repaired, as the ocean's (id's) power will continue to beat against our (ego) defenses. The work of psychoanalysis, akin to Maimonides' Guide's search for wisdom and love of God, is a lifelong task. It is asymptotic in that we can hew closer and closer to a more noble inner life and complementary actions, living. Further, Freud cautioned that even if we perform a meticulous job of interpretation, including infantile origins, there is some point in the dream we may not interpret "completely," the "navel of the dream."[3] This reminds us of Maimonides' caution that because man is corporeal—has needs and desires of the flesh (hunger, sex, sleep), man is limited in his striving for full wisdom (Stern, 2013).

We note another parallel between the Guide and the dream book, between Maimonides and Freud. We noted earlier that Maimonides called the Guide "my opinions" and suggested that this was a deeply personal work. So, too, Freud confides, "For this book has a further subjective significance for me personally ... It was, I found, a portion of my own self-analysis, my reaction to my father's death ... Having discovered that this was so, I felt unable to obliterate the traces of the experience" (1900, p. xxvi).

Grubrich-Simitis concludes, "With self-assured emphasis, Freud ... defines *The Interpretation of Dreams* as his most personal book, and indeed as a work of quasi-autobiography." (Grubrich-Simitis, 2000, pp. 1164–1165).

A father's death is the nucleus for self-analysis and the subsequent dream book. A brother's death, we argue, was the nucleus for the *Guide*, completed for a student who left too soon.

Nevertheless, we interpret, we work asymptotically. Let's start that journey by reviewing Freud's classic.

We lay the foundation to study the dream book, by recognizing how personal is this account, by studying the process by which it developed.

Before we enter this dream book, before we listen in on Freud's dreams, let us review the history of how this book came about, including its "pre-history" and its evolution as part of the genre of "autobiography" initiated by Rousseau.

In a previous book (Szajnberg, 2023), I articulated in the chapter on Rousseau, autobiography and Freud, how the literary genre of (written) "autobiography" was initiated by Rousseau's *The Confessions*, including his confession that he wrote this book to ameliorate his "sins" for which he feels both guilt and shame (Szajnberg, in press). I point out in that chapter that Rousseau gives at least six reasons for his shame, but the reader finds many more "sins" to which he confesses throughout the work. Further, Rousseau's *Confessions* were precipitated by the harsh, personal critique of a former friend, Voltaire. While readers may cite Augustine as the author of the first *Confessions*, Augustine's aim, in contrast, was to show how Christ was present from early days in Augustine's life to guide him from sin to holiness; it is not a developmental study like Rousseau's (Szajnberg, op. cit.). Cellini also falls within this realm of not only "confessing" his sins (including murder) but more so regaling us in his antics, without attention to his developmental origins. Others may point out that Montaigne's *Essays* (Montaigne, 2006; Baudry, 2022, personal communication) were also self-reflection, if not developmentally autobiographical, with which we agree and perhaps Rousseau would also concur. In sum, Rousseau is a pioneer in developmental, harsh, self-reflection. He initiated a genre that Freud developed but in an oral-aural medium.

Dreaming on a Hard Bench

How did Freud come about writing what he confesses is his most personal work?

Grubrich-Simitis (2000) offers a painstaking review of the numerous editions, Freud's correspondence with Fliess, with Freud's wife and others that tell us the profound efforts and his fundamental decision to use his own dreams to illustrate his book.

We now know that while this book's publication date is 1900, it was finished and promised to be published for Fliess's birthday in 1899.

Long after its publication, Freud once asserted that the book was already finished in all essentials by 1896 but had been written out only in the summer of 1899 (Freud, 1914, p. 22). The Fliess letters from 1895 on do in fact document Freud's collecting of dream texts and interpretations and the making of his first hypotheses, sometimes interwoven with the traces of his incipient self-analysis and meandering back and forth between these two processes. For example, the letter of September 23, 1895 already includes the central thesis "that dreams are motivated by wish fulfilment" (1985, p. 140). Freud's dream "Close the eyes/an eye", which he had on the night after his father's funeral and which, with some modifications, he later discussed in *The Interpretation of Dreams* (Freud, 1900, p. 218), is recorded in the letter of November 2, 1896 (1985, p. 202). Again, the letter of October 15, 1897 contains an anticipatory, as yet private, sketch of the concept of the Oedipus complex (Cohler, 2015): he touched upon for the first time publicly in his dream book, but in1897 he derived his ideas mainly from insights accruing from his self-analysis and his new understanding, closely connected with these, of the gripping power of the tragedies of Oedipus and Hamlet.

Further, we know that parts of the book were rapidly *written* over some weeks. Yet, the thinking of the book and some preliminary written efforts go back to at least 1893. For Freud, the book's *writing* was precipitated by: 1. His father's death; 2. Freud's analysis of his own dreams around his father's death with his discovery of his Oedipal complex; and 3. Freud's dialogue (via correspondence) with Fliess about these matters. We will return to these circumstances, but remind the reader that in the Maimonides chapter, we note that he began his monumental *Guide* shortly after the drowning death of his beloved brother, which left Maimonides bedridden and prostrate for at least a year. Such mourning is supposed to be prevented, if not prohibited, by the Jewish laws of mourning. We can at least note that from Maimonides' perspective, he too wrote these as a series of letters to his precious student, Joseph.

Freud's arduous efforts were a nocturnal affair, not only his dreaming, but also his writing down his dreams. He moved onto a harder surface to sleep in his library in order that he would awaken, better remember his dreams, and write them down along with their associations (Grubrich-Simitis, 2000, p. 1156).[4]

And Freud's dialogue with Fliess about this dream book was at times fraught with difficulties. In 1898, Fliess's critiques led to Freud's interrupted writing, "a stoppage, an inhibition" (Grubrich-Simitis, 2000, p. 1157), which resulted in complex revisions.

For all the efforts, Freud's book sold only some 600 copies over the next nine years. The publisher/bookseller continued to keep the copies available (unheard of today) until a second edition was issued a decade later.

Understanding the fuller meaning of the dream book—including infantile origins of the Irma dream—entails studying other literature surrounding its creation and revisions. The next seven editions, revised in Freud's lifetime, give hints of Freud's infantile origins for "Irma" as included in the Minutes of the Vienna Psychoanalytic Society (Nunberg and Federn, 1974). Herein, for example, Freud presented a dream, such as sliding down a smooth exterior with anxiety near the end, and requested comments from the Wednesday group. Several gave examples and ideas, some of which were included in subsequent editions of the dream book. With the Wednesday group, we introduce a lively version of dialogue (we suggest different from the correspondence with Freud's idealized Fliess) to Freud's thinking. We limn closer to Danté and Virgil, to Maimonides and his "Joseph" (or later, his letters of response to rabbis in Yemen, Provence, and so forth).

Yet, the dream book remains a deeply personal book, but not a solipsistic work: it has become a foundational text for psychoanalysts and even Western thought. This is a significant innovation: how an admittedly personal account of chthonic life is transformed by honest critical thinking. It becomes a guide for those perplexed by their dream life, their inner lives. It becomes a central text for understanding not only dreams, but also the mental mechanisms for concealing and revealing; the more valuable that lies beneath.

Let's now examine more closely first the cardinal "Irma" dream and then what Freud learns about inner life mental mechanisms from this and other dreams.[5]

The Irma dream covers two-thirds of a page, followed by *ten* pages of interpretation and a final discovery, not just of the latent (hidden) meaning of this dream, but also the motive and structure of all dreams as wishes and motives.

But we will also demonstrate, as with Maimonides' use of the *external* meanings of *Torah*, that manifest/external/parabolics are valuable in three ways: First, the external layer contains hints to the internal, hidden meanings. Second, the external meanings have value in and of themselves: to maintain societal equilibrium. Third, as Stern argues in Maimonides' use of parables, there may be limits to our understanding that parables indicate: even for Freud, there are points in the dream that are unplumbable, the navel.

That is, we can modify the analogy between external/internal, concealed/revealed, and "wheat/chaff." At first, we suggested that the wheat is the more valuable inner meaning and the chaff is the lesser meaning. But we will explore how both with Maimonides and Freud, the external has an inherent value. We will review Erik Erikson's (1954) remarkable, at the time provocative, study[6] of the Irma dream: that external meaning, the manifest dream, also has a value that helps us discern further meaning in the dream.

The Specimen Dream

"Preamble[7]

...I had been giving psycho-analytic treatment to a young lady ... friendly ... with. my family ... a source of many disturbed feelings.... the physician's...authority is less...

This treatment had ended in a partial success;...I proposed a solution ...which she seemed unwilling to accept. ...we had broken off the treatment for the summer ...—

...I had a visit from ...(Otto), one of my oldest friends, who had been staying with ..., Irma, and her family... he answered: 'She's better, but not quite well....Otto's words, ... annoyed me.....(M)y patient's relatives,... had never ... favour(ed) ... the treatment. (M)y disagreeable impression was not clear to me....

(That) ... evening I wrote out Irma's case history, (for)... Dr. M. (a common friend)... to justify myself. ...... I had the following dream...

...

'A large hall—numerous guests,...—Among them ... Irma. I at once took her on one side, ... to answer her letter ... to reproach her for not having accepted my 'solution'.... I said... 'If you still get pains, it's really only your fault.' She replied: 'If you only knew what pains I've got now in my throat and stomach and abdomen—it's choking me' —I was alarmed.... She looked pale and puffy. I thought ... that ...I must be missing ... organic trouble. I took her to the window and looked down her throat, ... she showed signs of recalcitrance, like women with artificial dentures. I thought... there was really no need for her to do that.—She then opened her mouth properly ... on the right I found a big white patch; at another place I saw extensive whitish grey scabs upon ...curly structures...(like nasal)... turbinal bones....—I at once called in Dr. M., ... he repeated the examination. ... Dr. M. looked quite different ... very pale, ... limp(ed) ... chin ... clean-shaven.... My friend Otto was now standing beside her ... and my friend Leopold was percussing her through her bodice ...: 'She has a dull area low down on the left.' ... a portion of the skin on the left shoulder was infiltrated.(I noticed this,..., in spite of her dress.) ... M. said: '...no doubt it's an infection, but no matter; dysentery will supervene and the toxin will be eliminated.' ... We were ... aware, ..., of the infection's origin. Not long before,... my friend Otto had given her an injection ...of propyl, propyls ... propionic acid ... trimethylamin (... I saw ... the formula...) ... Injections of that sort ought not to be made so thoughtlessly. ... the syringe had not been clean.'"

Freud continues with his interpretation, some ten pages in English. To paraphrase him, he "immediately" recognizes the previous day's events that precipitated the dream: a visit from his close friend Otto, who has been staying with the Irma family and reports she is not well. Freud feels reproached. That evening he writes up the case in order to send it to their mutual friend Dr. M. Freud notes that Irma's "dream" symptoms differ from those with which she presented. He finds it amusing that in the dream Irma gets a "senseless" injection and Dr. M's consoling response. The end of the dream seemed "more obscure and compressed" (Freud, op. cit.).

We are not here to reanalyze Freud's dream, although we will call into play further biographical information of childhood residues that make more sense of this specimen dream (Cohler, 2015) and also Erikson's (1954) thoughtful exploration of the manifest dream in order to explain better why *this man* at *this time* published, in fact publicized, *this dream*.

Rather, our intent in this chapter consistent with this book is to first artic-ulate the mechanisms of dream work, later the techniques to uncover the hid-den meanings, and at the same time note how these parallel Maimonides' findings and techniques of concealed/revealed. In this sense, both Freud and Maimonides are clarifying techniques of thought when it comes to deeply important, emotionally charged topics—whether it be the inner life of the Torah or the inner life of our dreams.

For instance, let's start with what might appear to be insignificant words. From the phrase, "I at once called on Dr. M...", Freud extracts two words "at once." A naive reader (as we are without *his* associations) might pass over these relatively neutral two words. Instead, Freud's point is:

> "... 'at once' was sufficiently striking to require a special exploration."
> Then, he associates to "a tragic event in my practice" about the death of a patient (with the same name as his eldest daughter; who died several years later).

"At once," we might say, has a tenor similar to the *Torah*'s "Hineini," here I am. "Here I am" seems a straightforward phrase to the naive reader. But to those who know its use in *Torah*, we recall that whenever a character says this one word—which Alter (2019) calls a "pointing word"— a momen-tous, even (almost) tragic event will occur: Abraham almost sacrifices Isaac; Joseph agrees to his father's request to oversee his brothers' work, almost killed by his brothers, is instead sold into slavery (to Ishmael's heirs) and thought dead by his father, and so on. Even Moses, when God calls his name from the burning bush, answers with only one word, "Hineini," "Here I am" (Alter, 2019, Gen 3:4). We recall Maimonides' admonishment that to grasp the secrets (of *Torah*, of the *Guide*) we should pay attention to simple words that appear to be in passing, such as "seemingly," "almost," and "perhaps."

Representation

Representation is our most significant category both for Freud and Maimonides. Freud tells us what we already realize: almost all dreams are visual representations. Only occasionally do we hear speech in dreams and when this happens, it is often something overheard during the day. But dreams are *Bilder*, pictures, moving pictures. And when they also move us emotionally, we remember them.

Freud put "representation" as the last of three techniques of dream work. Yet, the *visual* representation is fundamental to dreaming; we will suggest that then subsequent two techniques—displacement and condensation—are derived from the visual quality of dreams. You will see that Freud gives multiple examples of *visual* displacement and condensation. This will connect us back to Maimonides' two centrally visual topics of the *Guide*, the Creation and the Chariot.

Yet, "words" can be condensed. "Words in dreams are treated as thought they were things" (p. 299). Freud persuades us, in dream interpretation, to "treat words like objects" as children do. There is an ambiguity in the child's mind (in the dream mind) between "word" and "thing." This again reminds us of the ambiguity in the Hebrew "dvr" which Maimonides uses—the lexical ambiguity of word and thing.

I return for the moment to Maimonides two, and only two, subjects of the *Guide:* the Creation and the Chariot. Both are, of course, written texts; because they were written, they have endured with little change (unlike oral texts).[8] Yet, they mean to describe two eminently *visual* experiences: Creation and Ezekiel's visions. The creation story is highly visual: from a background of *tohu v'vohu*,[9] a blank screen of darkness, of void, we "see" appear before our very "eyes" a world, a sky, water, land, animals that fly, crawl, swim, and finally man and woman. Yet it is also true that the word has primacy. God speaks: "y'hi or!," let there be light, or "p'ru u'rvu" "be fruitful and multiply!" (This is the first ever commandment God gives to beings (animals), as opposed to the enduring non-living things such as light or water.) This laconic God does visual marvels with speech: his "words" *(d'varim)* make "things" *(d'varim)*. Return to Maimonides' citation of Proverbs 25:

"God's honor is to hide a matter,/The honor of kings to plumb a matter."

Followed several verses later by:

"Golden apples (with)in ornamental silver/words are spoken before his face"

From these two verses, Maimonides abstracts an explanation: the well-written/spoken phrase has multiple meanings; one should hearken to the words *(but)* listen with the heart. This could be advice to a psychoanalyst and analysand.

In an uncanny touch, the dark screen upon which God visually (and physically) creates sky, waters, land, animals ... man, I suggest conjuring up two remarkable psychoanalytic papers on the visual and even sensual dream representations of the "background" screen for dreaming. Isakower (1938) reported dreamers' account of a descending three-dimensional image that flattens and fills the mouth, occasionally with prickling or needle-like sensations. Lewin, building on this, reports a visual image that precedes the dream of something blank that flattens out upon which the dream scenes are then "projected" (Lewin, 1948). While this chapter and book concentrate on Freud's dream book (rather than later dream literature, which is voluminous), we cannot read Maimonides' Creation account and the *Torah* account itself of God's *tohu v'vohu* as the screen upon which He projects His creations.

Displacement (Upward)

Here's upward displacement (anatomically). Freud's self-analysis entailed lengthy correspondence with Fliess. Flies had extensive, even fantastical, beliefs about how the nasal cavity was "connected" with particularly female sexual dysfunction. He surgerized woman's nasal cavities to "repair" their hysterical—genital—symptoms. One such patient was referred by Freud and Freud traveled to Berlin to surgically assist: the woman returned to Vienna, almost dying because Fliess had left surgical packing within the wound (Cohler, 2015). Knowing this, we can reread the passage in the Irma dream that goes as follows:

"She then opened her mouth properly and on the right I found a big white patch; at another place I saw extensive whitish grey scabs upon some remarkable curly structures which were evidently modeled on the *turbinal bones of the nose*" *(Author's italics)*. These nasal turbinal passages, even extensive scabs, are displacements from the mucous-secreting rugae of the vagina (and stomach). The "scabs" suggest a healing wound or infection, not a healthy orifice. (Much like the real infection that Fliess incurred in this hapless woman's nasal cavities, while "curing" her vaginal symptoms.) Hence, we have two displacements: 1. "upwards" performed in the dream work. We make "acceptable" in the manifest dream by shifting the turbinates of the vagina upward (nonsensically as it may seem) to the nose, or the mouth/throat; 2. a displacement from the purulent white packing in Fliess's (Freud's) patient that was left in *her* turbinates; a displacement from one patient to another, *and* a displacement of culpability.

And, just in case the reader is not certain that propyl/amyl/turbinates refer to the feminine anatomy, later (p. 294 ff) Freud tells us that "propyl" leads to "amyl" which leads to Fliess's idiosyncratic ideas about the female chemical/sexual processes. Another tip-off? The word "propylaea" that Freud "sees" in his dream refers to the Athenian ceremonial portico of a structure: that "entrance" way into a house, that feminine reception/receptacle.

The reader will recall one hiding technique by Maimonides: put contradictions in two different places in a text so that one denies the other. This—nasal turbinates—*isn't* about vaginas, the dreamer can say; it is just throats and noses, so to speak. That is, displacement of covertly contradictory thoughts is a mental technique of concealing. And yet, the nonsensical nature of the manifest dream *demands* of Freud (or us, to our desire for logic, for explanation) to question; what's this about—this nasal turbinate stuff, or this dullness in the lower left chest, or this infiltrate? Even injections make more sense if they are sexual injections as suggested by the associa-tions as Freud progresses from "propyl, propyls ... propionic acid ... tri-methylamin"; "Trimethylamin was an allusion not only to the immensely powerful factor of sexuality, but also to a person whose agreement I recalled with satisfaction ..." (p. 117). This is a progression from something toxic to something semen-ish even (which for some women felt toxic). Another method to contradict, as Maimonides listed, is to contradict by omission (or addition): in this case, the dreamer "omits" the vaginal cavity, overtly insisting he is only visualizing diseased throats or nasal turbinates.[10]

In the next 13 pages of "Analysis," Freud guides us meticulously through the major revealing elements of the dream, toward understanding the mind of the dreamer. He even italicizes the key phrases that are like *hermes*, markers, along this journey from inchoate puzzlement to clarity. I will cite a few such marker phrases before turning to Chapter 6, in which Freud summarizes the major techniques of dream work to conceal meaning and consequently the interpretive techniques to reveal the hidden treasures of meaning.

When we look at some of the key phrases, let us also recall Maimonides' techniques for concealment (in both his *Guide* and the *Torah*).

"She looked pale and puffy," in contradiction to the real Irma's rosy complexion.

"(F)alse teeth" leads us to two other women with whom Irma is compared unfavorably. Freud realizes he'd like to trade Irma for the (more compliant) others (p. 110).

"*'At once,' required a special explanation.... a tragic event in my practice* ..." (p. 111). Here again, we are drawn to Maimonides' insistence that *simple, even bland words can be key concealers.* The example above, *HineinI*, "Here I am," fits this specific association. Freud's "at once" directs him to a tragic death in his practice; Abraham's or Joseph's or Moses' "Hineini" precedes, even leads them to momentous, almost tragic episodes.

This next phrase leads Freud to greater candor with us and connects with Maimonides' use of parable to "explain" (Stern, 2013). Freud writes, "*In spite of her dress...,*" first alluding to physicians who examine children through their clothes, then a "celebrated physician" who examined clothed patients. Then Freud ends abruptly. "Frankly, I had no desire to penetrate more deeply at this point" (p. 113). We could speculate that Freud's use of "desire" and "penetrate" has something to do with sexual penetration that he won't pursue here. But whether we are correct or not, our point is that Maimonides first taught us that we may never achieve full wisdom and awe (of God) because we are made of matter, of flesh (Stern, 2013); there are limits to which we can achieve full(er) intelligence, both of God (per Maimonides) or of ourselves (per Freud). Both confess this truth: that we approach full knowledge asymptotically, and our limits are inherent to our being human. Nevertheless, both Maimonides and Freud urge us to pursue (self) knowledge as a lifelong effort, which in itself is fulfilling, ennobling.

Consider more closely Freud's "I had no desire to penetrate more deeply …" We recognize two different explanations for his coming up short on completing the interpretation. First, may be Freud's conscious decision not to reveal something personal that could harm his reputation (in his contemporary professional circles; with his reader). Second, might also be a connection to Freud's remark about the navel of the dream; that we approach a point in the dream that appears not further interpretable. From Maimonides' perspective, this is analogous to his use of parable (Stern, 2013): that because we are of flesh, the parable expresses meaning as best as we can approach, even though we may not achieve full understanding (at this moment, perhaps ever).

Condensation

This obscuring dream technique is related often to the third characteristic technique, visual representation (which we discuss below). The dream, like fine perfume, is a composite of many components. For instance, "Irma" represents: the patient Irma; Freud's daughter (with the membranous illness); Freud's patient who died of self-poisoning; child neurology patients; his daughter Sophie; his wife (reluctant to open her mouth); and others (throats). One can create composites in two ways. First, combine several figures into one combined image. For instance, Dr. M. possesses his own speech and behavior *but* has the face and the pale appearance of Freud's brother. Second, one can superimpose two facial appearances such that the common features are amplified and the differences disappear or are canceled. Dr. R. with his grey beard represents both Freud and his own father (Freud, 1900).

One additional visual technique in dreams, a form of condensation, is reversal of a dream thought's image. In fact, Freud notes, reversal is the most common (concealing) technique "…favored by dream work" (p. 327). For instance, the "bartloss" ("beardless") chin of Dr. M. could represent in fact a *bearded* character, such as Freud himself, or his father. This would be the use of omission or reversal: turning the beard into beardless is reversal, or omitting the beard would be the disguise by omission. I use the terms used by Maimonides to continue our comparisons of concealing/revealing techniques.

Chapter Six and Dream's Work Techniques Expanded

In Chapter 6, Freud writes about the relationship between dream content and dream thoughts: that ego work during sleep transforms the original thought into dream content *in order to disguise the unacceptable wishes* underlying the dream thoughts. There is a censor operating during dream formation.

In fact, Freud writes, reminiscent of Maimonides, the overall principle he discovers is that *dream content doesn't equal or is even inverse to the original dream thoughts.* Recall here that one of Maimonides' first major efforts in the *Guide* is to "prove" that God has no body, despite multiple passages in Torah that speak of God's body or finger or hand or foot, even that man is made in the image of God. Borrowing Freud's terms, Maimonides argues that *Torah* "content" conceals *Torah's* underlying "thoughts."

Freud demonstrates with examples:

1 The Botanical Flowers monograph dream's (manifest) *content* is flowers, dried or photographed, but the analysis reveals that the (latent) dream *thoughts* are about collegial conflict and even Freud's *dislike* of botany (p. 285).
2 The Sappho dream's *content* is ascending/descending, but the dream *thoughts* are about the danger of sex with social inferiors[11] (p. 285).
3 The May beetles dream's *content* is cruelty to beetles; the *thoughts* are about the cruelty of sex (p. 289).
4 The Uncle dream's *content* a fair-bearded fellow; the *thoughts* are about Freud's ambitious wishes (136 ff).

Here is an example from Freud on the use of *contradiction and derision* (p. 426 ff) using plays on one word, "fahren." We cite this example as it also shows, as with Maimonides, how meticulous Freud suggests we need to understand "a" word: one must not only look at the word itself, but also its context.

The dream in brief followed Freud's meeting with Count Thun: *Freud is "fahren" ("driving") in a cab; asking the cabbie to stop at a railway station. The driver complains he was overtired. It seems as if Freud had driven him the distance one usually "fahren" ("traveling") by train.*

In his analysis, Freud notes that the word "fahren" can mean either (active) driving a cab or (passive) traveling on a train. But "fahren" is also an ambiguous word in a childhood riddle, that is the root of *Vorfahren*, meaning either "driven up" (concretely) or "ancestry" (more meaningfully) for this dream.[12] The second part of the riddle's answer is "Nachkommen," meaning "follow after" (concretely) or "progeny" (more meaningfully) (p. 431 ff). The "absurd" dream content about a cab or train travel and complaining cabbie evolves via associations to the dream thoughts having to do with ancestors and progeny.

What is *not* represented can be meaningful. The *form* of the dream may give hints as to its meaning. An example Freud gives is a dream in which the dreamer reports "gaps" in the dream's forms. On analysis, these "gaps" were key to understanding what the male dreamer had in mind: as a child (and in his adulthood dreaming), the dreamer considered vaginas as "gaps," something "missing" in the woman, something damaged. Here, Freud uses the manifest form of the (un)remembered gaps as the key to the dream.[13] I ask the reader to keep a parallel track in mind with Maimonides, specifically his use of "omission" to conceal/reveal truths.

Emotions, the Dream, Maimonides' Torah

Freud's section on emotion *(der Affekt)* in dreams is relatively short 25 pages (462–487) compared to even the rest of Chapter 6, some 232 pages. But brevity does not equal lesser importance (in Freud, in dreams, in Maimonides). For, Freud begins, affects are like the motor which propels dreams, giving them their charge: if dream thoughts and their unconscious revisions result in dream content, then affects are the acceleration and velocity we experience during the nighttime ride. Dreams are Ezekiel's Chariot ride to our inner otherworldly spheres.

But, first a detour into the complexity, even ambiguity, the slipperiness of the words "emotion," "affect/affekt," and "feeling." In English and German, these words often are used interchangeably. They should not be. "Feeling" can include sensations such as the reader's *derrier* as she reads this, a chill breeze, or exhaustion, as well as a host of "emotions." "Affect" is a more abstract, emotionally-removed term. "Emotions," since Darwin's now classic *The Expression of Emotions in Man and Animal* (1872), postulated six basic, universal (human) emotions: anger, fear, surprise, disgust, happiness, and sadness, although postulating other possible emotions. Over a century later, Ekman and colleagues demonstrated empirically that at least the seven basic emotions *are* universal with typical facial expressions (for all but shyness).[14] In his 2003 work, Ekman postulates up to 12 or 13 universal emotions, including *Schadenfreude*,[15] *naches*,[16] *fiero*,[17] awe,[18] desire, embarrassment, sympathy, and others (Cordaro et al., 2018).

"Emotion" derives from the Latin word, *motus*, which means move, or move out, motion, movement, for it gives us the sense of being moved internally (without external voluntary muscle movement[19]). Even Freud's German *der Affekt* captures the subjective sense of "movement" in one of its synonyms, *die Bewegung* ("movement" or "motion"). For this chapter, we will use "Affect," although we'd prefer "emotion," in order to remain consistent with Freud's term, *der Affekt*.[20]

Freud begins his study of affects in dreams with a clear statement, *".ideational material has undergone displacements and substitutions, whereas the **affects have remained unaltered**" (p. 460). Or, "affect experienced in a dream is in no way inferior to one of equal intensity experienced in waking life" (p. 460 ff).* The dream book is focused on how our manifest dreams, our dream *contents*, are transformed, morphed, by the force of the dream censor, from the original dream *thoughts*, in order to disguise unacceptable wishes. The fundamental cognitive nature of dreams is that they are[21] changed. But Freud claims, at first, affects "remain unaltered." The affect connected in the remembered visual content is "true" because it is in fact connected to a (hidden) true dream thought.

And then, Freud surprises us again (reminding us of Maimonides' working both sides of the street), as he states "....dream work brings about a suppression of affects" (p. 462). Wait, didn't he just say the opposite—"affects are unaltered"? Freud continues that one of the mechanisms with which dreams are made involves changing affects to their opposite (p. 471). In fact,

> ..."*inhibition of affect, (is)... the second consequence of the censorship of dreams, just as dream-distortion is its first* ..."
>
> (p. 468)

Which is true: are affects *unchanged* or are they *inhibited, transformed, or turned into the opposite* (of which Freud gives examples)? Well, both are true. If we listen to the process by which affects are first experienced in dreams, then how they are transposed by displacement onto a dreamed visual object, distracting us away from the original object, then the affect is the same, and different. An analogy is how physicists think of light as waves and particles. It depends.

A few pages later, as if to beg the reader's indulgence, Freud explains (while dissecting his own dream of "Grauen") "gruesome" or "greying":

> "The dissection meant the self-analysis ... carried out in the publication of this ... book about dreams—(This has) been so distressing to me ... that I had postponed the ...finished manuscript for more than a year. A wish then arose that I might get over this feeling of distaste; hence it was that I had no gruesome feeling ['Grauen'] in the dream. But I should also have been very glad to miss growing grey—'Grauen' in the other sense of the word. (But)...the grey of my hair was another reminder that I must not delay any longer. ...the thought that I should have to leave it to my children to reach the goal of my difficult journey forced its way through to representation at the end of the dream."
>
> (pp. 477–478)

Freud may not be the only one distressed by this process; the reader may join his distress to understand the nature of affects/emotions in dreams.

He regains our indulgence, our patience with him, when he concludes:

> "...to interpret and report one's dreams demands a high degree of self-discipline. One is bound to emerge as the only villain among the crowd of noble characters who share one's life."
>
> (p. 489)

We are not here to villainize him for the twists and turns of understanding our chthonic lives; perhaps we will be patient, possibly even praise him in a pantheon of "noble characters who share one's life," a pantheon of few, including Solomon's *Kohelet*, Danté, Montaigne, Rousseau.

Dream emotions remain "true" to the original dream thought; emotion may be inhibited, transformed, and connected to a different dreamed thought (content) to which the emotion feels foreign, for it is. Emotion is both unchanged and yet can be changed. It depends.

With this, we leave the overview of Freud's dream book, aiming only to establish the commonalities with Maimonides' *Guide*. Both are:

1 Highly visual (dream content; Creation/Chariot) and replete with movement;
2 Have layered meanings;
3 Whose manifest, external layers hint at hidden and more meaningful latent, internal layers;
4 The narrative (*Guide*/dream) transforms the vibrant visual into the more shadowy words, words that struggle to capture the vibrancy of the visual;
5 The external, manifest material (dream or narrative) contains embedded within hints to the hidden meanings;
6 Paradoxically, there is ambivalence built into the manifest, external text: *what is concealed is done so in such a manner that it can be revealed*;
7 There are *specific techniques to conceal/reveal*. For Freud, these are representation (predominately visual); displacement; condensation. These include subcategories of omission, addition, superimposing several images to both amplify and disguise features, and so on. For Maimonides, he lists (detailed in our previous chapters) that he will use mostly contradictions, but he has at least six different ways to do this, including omission or addition. He also uses parable, even as he states that he will not do this as this would duplicate the *Torah*. And, Maimonides' parable is uniquely defined: it is something that tries to express in words what may be inexpressible ultimately (Stern, op. cit.). We draw an analogy to Freud's idea of the navel of a dream.

With this, let us turn to thinking about what this medieval physician and that *fin-de-siécle* physician teach us about the workings of our inner lives.

Notes

1 "…children in the screen memory were in fact his nephew John and his niece Pauline, who appear at several points in The Interpretation of Dreams (1900a). (Cf., for instance, Standard Ed., **5**, **424-5**, **483** and **486**.)"
2 Freud and Emma Ekstein went to Berlin for Fliess's surgery. Fliess apparently "inadvertently" left surgical packing in the nasal cavity that resulted in near-death and multiple surgical repairs in Vienna.
3 'There is at least one spot in every dream at which it is unplumbable—a navel, as it were, that is its point of contact with the unknown' (Freud, Interpretation of Dreams, 1900, p. 111, n. 1/p. 76).
4 "…in 1895, reported in passing that, having found himself obliged to exchange his usual bed for a harder one, he had had particularly frequent and vivid dreams and had taken the trouble to write them down and 'try to solve them'

(Freud and Breuer, 1895 p. 69, n). This was probably in 1893, as the following sentence from a letter to Minna Bernays dated 17 April that year suggests: 'I am in fact sleeping in the library room and can make the finest studies of noteworthy dreams'. Ten days later, in another letter to his sister-in-law, he writes: 'I am now using my sleep in the library room to note down my dreams; this will yield a fine piece of work … in 10 years' time'."

5   Another parallel with Maimonides.

Maimonides tells the reader/listener that *all he is about to unveil* he came about *through his own learning*; he did not learn the matters of the *Guide* from others (although he is grateful to several of his father's teachers).

So too, *Freud learned about his dreams* (and consequently about dreams) *from his self*, his self-analysis. Much of the first chapter of the dream book is his almost obsessive recounting of previous dream literature … and their uselessness.

This could sound narcissistic. But then we would have to consider Archimides' discoveries, or Galileo's discoveries, or Tycho Brahe's, or Harvey's circulation discovery, or Einstein's also "narcissistic" … *and* universal.

6   Anna Freud, objecting to anyone writing about her father's dream, blocked the publication of Erikson's cardinal study for several years. It was finally published in the Journal of the American Psychoanalytic Association.

7   For copyright reasons, we have quoted under 400 words of the 552-word section. When an English word may not capture the full ambiguity of the German, I will footnote. The preamble and Freud's interpretation I abbreviate using boldface type to highlight significant features.

8   See the 2022 review of the new *Gilgamesh* epic for a discussion of the importance of Assyrian writing's endurance, particularly under the buried sands of time. This is contrasted with the shifting translations of Homer's oral epic prior to its being written (Macfarlane, R. NYRB October 2022).

9   Fox was troubled by these unclear Hebrew words. He settled on chaos and confusion. He uses these words to connect with the later Prophets. Alter uses "welter and waste and darkness."

10 There is a spatial transformation in the Irma dream that was elaborated by L. Balter (2020). Freud's dream begins in a large hall. After some steps, the space narrows down to a woman's mouth, throat, and nasal turbinates. And, as Balter documents, spatial transformations in dreams are often associated with regressions. We begin and move from a large hall populated by Freud's acquaintances to nasal turbinates and associated more regressive sexual matters. In the large hall, Freud is receiving others, acquaintances; in the turbinates, Freud is intruding on a more intimate space. As Freud did with Fliess in Emma's nasal turbinates, packing it with something they forgot to remove, almost killing the woman. Other references to dream space transformations and their meanings can be found in Erikson (1954) and Roth and Blatt (1974).

11 (Let's keep in mind that Ezekiel's Chariot vision is all about ascending and descending. Like Aristotle's "man" hopping heavenward, then being brought back to earth.)

12 See Freud (1900, p. 434) for the association's elegant cacophony play on *fahren* words from *verhergefahren (driven before)* to *vorgefahren (*driven up) to *Vorfahren* (ancestry), dreamt in that order.

13 Ironically, this was key to Erik Erikson's "controversial" paper interpreting Freud's Irma dream (which, as mentioned, was blocked from publication by his former analyst, Anna Freud). Erikson relies on the richness of the dream's form including spatial representation, as the dreamer tells us something about dream thoughts. Freud preceded Erikson, as is typical of Freud's heterodox/orthodox genius (Frattaroli, 1992).

14 John Bowlby was so influenced by Darwin that Bowlby's final book was a biography of him (1990).
15 Freud gives plenty of personal examples of his own *Schadenfreude* toward others such as the Irma dream (p. 109 ff) among others (e.g., p. 193).
16 *Naches* is the Yiddish for a sense of pride in one's offspring or students' success.
17 *Fiero* is the Italian for a sense of personal success, a "personal best."
18 "Awe," we will discuss later, is a central emotion for Maimonides to harness to intellect in the pursuit of God and all *that* entails internally. "Awe" is a rare emotion (Ekman, 2003).
19 We do have unconscious or preconscious muscle movement such as in our faces.
20 We discuss details of "emotions" definition and their presence in *Torah* and dream books (both the narrative characters' emotions and the listener's responses). For now, we offer six characteristics of emotions: 1. An automatic appraisal; 2. Influenced by evolutionary and personal pasts; 3. Sensing something important to one's welfare; 4. With a set of (sometimes consciously) felt physiological and behavioral actions (within .20 seconds); 5. To deal with the situation; and 6. "...cannot be reduced to words" (Ekman, 2003, p. 13 ff). Even congenitally blind children, for instance, show the same facial expressions for specific emotions (Ekman, ibid., p. 14).
    We cite Freud's earliest (1894) "definition" of *affekt* to compare: "affect ... or sum of excitation—a quantity ... capable of increase, diminution, displacement and discharge, ... spread over the memory-traces of ideas somewhat as an electric charge is spread over the surface of a body'." And we recall that the last chapter of the dream book was written first, in the early 1890s). While we know that Freud read Darwin, we do not know if he read the *Expression of Emotions in Man and Animals*. We hope some Freud scholars will examine this.
21 The reader notes my phrasing "they are changed" as if our dreams were changed by some outside force. In fact, after Freud, we would be truer to say "we change our dreams." Yet, both are true: subjectively we feel as if our dreams "are changed"; only after analysis do we recognize that "*we* have changed" our dreams.

References

Alter, R. (2019). *The Art of Biblical Narrative*. Princeton.
Anzieu, D. (1986). *Freud's Self-Analysis, trans*. P. Graham. I.U.P.
Balter, L. (2020). The Nicholas Young Phenomenon. *IJP Open - Open Peer Review and Debate*, 7:1–33.
Baudry, F. (2022). On Michel Montaigne. Personal communication.
Bellow, S. (2008). *Humboldt's Gift*. Penguin.
Bowlby, J. (1990). *Charles Darwin, A Biography London*. Hutchinson.
Cohler, B. (2015). Reading *the Interpretation of Dreams: Freud and the Rhetoric of Wish and Awareness*. *Annu. Psychoanal.*, 38:20–39.
Cordaro, Daniel T., Sun, Rui, Keltner, Dacher, Kamble, Shanmukh, Huddar, Niranjan and McNeil, Galen. (February 2018). Universals and Cultural Variations in 22 Emotional Expressions across Five Cultures. *Emotion*, 18(1):75–93.
Ekman, P. (2003). *Emotions Revealed*. Holt.
Erikson, E. H. (1954). The Dream Specimen of Psychoanalysis. *Journal of the American Psychoanalytic Association*, 2:5–56
Fliess, W. (1902). *Über den ursächlichen Zusammenhang von Nase und Geschlechtsorgan: Zugleich ein Beitrag zur Nervenphysiologie. Halle an der* Saale, Carl Marhold.

Frattaroli, E. (1992). Heterodoxy and Orthodoxy in Freud. In: Szajnberg, N. (ed.) *Educating the Emotions: Bruno Bettelheim and Psychoanalytic Development*. Plenum.

Freud, S. (1895). *Project for a Scientific Psychology*. S. E., 1: 295–391. Hogarth Press, 1966.

Freud, S. (1899). *Screen Memories*. S. E. 3: 303–322. Hogarth Press, 1962.

Freud, S. (1900). *The Interpretation of Dreams*. S. E. 4. Hogarth Press.

Freud, S. (1914). *On the History of the Psychoanalytic Movement*. S. E. 14. p. 22. Hogarth Press.

Freud, S. (1925). *An Autobiographical Study*. S.E. 20. Hogarth Press.

Freud, S. (1933). New Introductory Lectures on Psycho-Analysis. *The Standard Edition of the Complete Psychological Works of Sigmund Freud*, 22:1–182.

Freud, S. and Brueuer, J. (1895). *Studies on Hysteria*. S. E. 2. P. 69.

Giovacchini, P. L. (2000). *The Impact of Narcissism*. Aronson.

Grinstein, A. (1968). *Sigmund Freud's Dreams*. I. U. P.

Grubrich-Simitis, I. (2000). Metamorphoses of the Interpretation of Dreams: Freud's Conflicted Relations with His Book of the Century. *Int. J. Psychoanal.*, 81:1155–1183.

Grubrich-Simitis, I. (2002). How Freud Wrote and Revised His Interpretation of Dreams: Conflicts around the Subjective Origins of the Book of the Century. *Psychoanalysis and History*, 4:111–126.

Isakower, O. (1938). A Contribution to the Patho-Psychology of Phenomena Associated with Falling Asleep. *International Journal of Psychoanalysis*, 19:331–345.

Lear, J. (2005). *Freud*. Routledge.

Lewin, B. D. (1948). Inferences from the Dream Screen. *Int. J. Psychoanal.*, 29:224–231.

Montaigne, M. (2006). Essays. Project Gutenberg.

Nunberg, H. and Federn, E. (1974). *Minutes of the Vienna Psychoanalytic Society*. Vol I–IV. IUP.

Roth, D. and Blatt, S. J. (1974). Spatial Representations and Psychopathology. *J. Am. Psychoanal. Assoc.*, 22:854–872.

Stern, D. (1985). *The Interpersonal World of the Infant*. Basic Books.

Stern, D. (2010). *Forms of Vitality*. Oxford University Press.

Stern, J. (2013). *The Matter and Form of Maimonides' Guide*. Harvard.

Szajnberg, N., Skrinjaric, J., and Moore, A. (1989). Affect Attunement, Attachment, Temperament and Zygosity: A Twin Study. *J. American Academy of Child and Adolescent Psychiatry*, 28:2, 249–253.

Szajnberg, N. (2023). *Psychic Mimesis: From Bible to Homer to Now*. Lexington.

Szajnberg, N. M. (1992). Psychoanalysis as an extension of autobiographical genre: Poetry and truth, fiction and reality. *Int. Rev. Psycho-Anal.*, 19: 375–87.

Denoumént: Rambam's Perplexing *Moreh* and Freud's Perplexing Dreams

What were they studying, trying to decipher—Rambam and Freud—that we could even consider are comparable subjects?

Their precious texts differed: for Rambam, the *Torah;* for Freud, dreams, mostly his. Yet, to each, their texts were the most precious to them personally.

But their aims converge. For, Rambam believed and aimed to demonstrate that greater pursuit of *Torah* results in a higher form of intellect and of being (even asymptotically along the path). For Freud, grasping the meaning of our inner life via dreams will enrich our inner lives; for "neurotics," even improve their lives. Both thinkers study in order to ennoble, elevate our ways of living. Ultimately, we achieve self-knowledge, for sure via Freud, but even via Rambam as we learn about the possibilities of how we can live better (believe and think better, for the *Guide*) despite our human, fleshy limits.

Still, the reader might argue, their "texts" were different. For Rambam, he wrote about only two sections of *Tanach*—the Creation and the Chariot—not even "all" of *Torah*. Also, Rambam's were *external* texts. Freud studied his own dreams and those of others.

Yet, I suggest we look more closely at these "texts," "texts" that are both — Torah and dreams—related in oral form even the sing-song, cantilled Torah; neither Torah (except the Ten Commandments written in stone) and certainly not dreams were originally in written form. And, both texts were highly precious to them: Rambam's *Torah*; Freud's "royal road to the unconscious."[1]

Rambam selects what he says are the two most puzzling secrets in the Torah,[2] leaving out perhaps the most precious secret, the tetragrammaton.[3] Both perplexing secrets are highly visual and highly moving and we also suggest highly emotional, for emotions move us. This is perhaps most obvious in Ezekiel's Chariot dream/visions: he is moved not only to Heaven and back, but moved emotionally by the, at moments, terrifying experiences. Rambam doesn't write about the whole of Ezekiel's prophecies. He picks out the most vivid, visual subjective experience in all *Tanach* (per Alter, but the reader can judge for himself). Alter (2019; Hosea (9:7)) has already

DOI: 10.4324/9781003358213-6

confessed to us, "The prophet is witless, the man of spirit crazed." And this Chariot is made to move us via Ezekiel, from earth-boundedness to the foot of God's throne. Even to the hand of God as he feeds and Ezekiel consumes the honey-tasting scroll. The Chariot itself is a *visual* feast. Recall:

> "...from within (a great cloud with fire flashing and radiance)...the likeness of four living creatures ...the likeness of a human being...each had four faces and four wings...straight legs and... the soles of a calf's foot, and they glittered like the look of burnished bronze. ...human hands beneath their wings on their four sides. And the faces and the wings of the four ...were joined to each other. ...the likeness of their faces, the face of a human and the face of a lion on the right of the four ...and the face of a bull to the left. and the face of an eagle to the four....(W) herever the spirit was to go, they would; they did not turn. ... (T)heir look was like burning coals....torches going back and forth among the creatures....radiance and...lightning came forth. And look,...one wheel was on the ground...the wheels ...were like chrysolite and a single likeness the faces of them had...a wheel is within a wheel. ...Their rims ...were fearsome and filled with eyes....Wherever the spirit was there to go, there they went...for the spirit of the creature was in the wheels..."
>
> (Alter, 2019; Ezekiel I: 4–21)

And at the pinnacle of Ezekiel's ascent, the ultimate vision, a vision denied to Moses, initiated by terrible sounds:

> "The sound of their wings like the sound of many waters, like the sound of Shaddai....an uproar, like the sound of an armed camp."
>
> (Alter, 2019; Ezekiel I:24-5)

Then to the vision:

> "...over their heads (the winged creatures), ...it was like the look of sapphire stone, the likeness of a throne and above...like a human form ... from the look of his loins above ...and below, I saw like the look of fire and radiance...the rainbow...the likeness of the glory of the Lord. And I saw and fell on my face..."
>
> (Alter, 2019; Ezekiel, 1:6–28)

As might *we* fall on our faces before such a maelstrom of vision and concatenation of sounds of wings, many waters, an uproar. This is not just "visual"; it is like an MGM Technicolor film, with Surround Sound, a vibrant color palette, much lightning and roaring, and much movement. The movement is physical (the wings, the wheels, the Chariot lifting us). The movement might also move the reader emotionally, like a dream/nightmare. We learn only in Chapter 3 *what* God commands Ezekiel to speak to the people of Israel. And in the next two chapters, we hear about the travails Ezekiel must endure before he can even deign to prophesize—such as lying on his left side for 390 days (to "bear the guilt of Israel") (Ezekiel, 4;6 ff), one day for each year of Israel's crime. And lying on his right side for 40 days for the "guilt of the house of Judah" alone. This is not enough preparation: he must shave his head and beard, then parse these into thirds and burn, strike and scatter them to the winds of Jerusalem.

Not until Chapters 6 and 7 does Ezekiel reveal to us, in part through poetry/song, what terrible things will befall the children of Israel. In Chapter 16, Ezekiel riffs on Isaiah, likening Israel to a whore. And the price Israel will pay for enjoying the "large members" of the Egyptians, Hittites, and others who pass their way, for opening her loins to them.

I give a more extended excerpt (only an excerpt, mind you) of this second secret that leads the studious Jew to perplexity, the Ezekiel Chariot passage that Rambam says is related to metaphysics, the study of the supra-lunar universe, the Divine. And *not* a study of metaphysics, he also proclaims. While brief, Ezekiel begins with a supra-lunar vision and even God's voice, a "study" of "metaphysics," which for Rambam is the study of the Divine science.

The reader might even recognize how dream-like (almost nightmarish) is Ezekiel's dream. One that might be amenable to Freud's interpretations.

But we need Ezekiel's associations, a problem that can be tackled methodologically (Szajnberg, 1992; Bettelheim, 2010).

Now, I return to the more familiar two Creation stories to recall how very visual and moving are these accounts. Because this is so familiar, my excerpts will be brief.

> "God *created* the heaven and earth and the earth was welter and waste and darkness of the deep and God's *breath* hovering over the waters, God *said*, "Let there be light." And there was light…. And God divided the light from the darkness. And God called the light Day and the darkness He called Night."
>
> (NS italics) (Genesis, I:1-3, Alter, 2019)

How visual! But I italicize verbs, actions, God takes sequentially to create a sensed universe: first "create," then "breath(e)," then" spoke." The Hebrew is clear: *before* God spoke any word, He somehow "created the heaven and earth." (Is this ברה barah a "thought" that precedes breath or words?) Then, his "wind" (רוח, *ru'ach*) (what we can also call "breath," that force that precedes and creates our words) hovers over the waters. This same breath, later called *n'shimah*, God uses to breathe life into Adam.[4] Only then does He speak—emit meaningful sounds, words—to create light. Almost like our own development, we create before words, then breath gives power to create our words, which, in turn, give names to what we create (although, unlike God, we do not believe our words in themselves create[5]). We have within two verses, Creation by some unspoken force (of heaven and earth), then riffling of waters by God's susurrating wind, and then his words, breaths that take form by our voices, our lips, and tongues. There is a final act: ours, when we hear these words of Creation, we create something. To paraphrase Sappho: words are mere air, but, when heard, are delicious (Hirsch, 2006).

I ask the reader to consider one's own act of speech. First, we have a thought that initiates the idea of a word, then the breath that we force through our vocal cords, past our tongue and lips until a word emerges. In infant research, Renee Spitz marveled at the infant's first verbal "no" around 12 months of age. It is an act of faith and self-assurance. Until then, when we press an undesirable morsel, perhaps broccoli, to the infant's lips, it will purse them, will even shake its head "no." Then, the infant who has enough faith in itself and in its caregiver will open its lips (a moment when an unempathic mother might force that morsel in) to say, "No," or even "No!"

Let's return to the movement and visualness of Creation. The Creation of man, for instance, is recapitulated. After a short introduction in Genesis I:27 "And God created the human in his image ... male and female He created them." We get a more detailed account in Chapter 2, and one in which there is flow among waters, wind, and humans, God shifts from a more distant "creator," *barah,* ברה, to *yatzar* יצר, "a craftsman, maker" (Alter, Genesis, p. 15 footnote). Here again, we note the movement and the visual.

> "...and wetness would well from the earth to water all the surface the soil, then the Lord God fashioned the human, humus from the soil and blew into his nostrils the breath of life..."

To capture the sensualness of the Hebrew, we use Alter's translation of "אדמה...אדמ" *adam* from *adamah* (earth or soil), we quote "יפח באפיו נשמת חיים...לנפש חיה" *yipach b'apav nishmat chaim, l'nefesh chaya,* the last two words could be translated "to a living (soulful[6]) creature." This is a more intimate act, creating and fashioning man: for his is made in God's image, and more intimately, God breathes life into man's nose, "inspires" man.

After planting the Tree of Knowledge, we hear (see) in four verses, more movement flow:

> "And a river came from Eden to water the garden and from there, splits and becomes four streams (literally, "heads")."
>
> (Alter, 2019; Genesis I:10 ff)

The reader might at first be struck with how wordy is this Creation story. But we remind ourselves that transforming the visual into words, as in the dream report, is a wordy enterprise: it takes many words to capture a moving image. Is an image worth a thousand words? If not precisely this number, we, like Borges (Borges, 2000; Szajnberg, 2013), can hear the exaggeration as an attempt to give heft to what we *see* in dreams, in visions. And the upwelling flow of water, followed by the flow of God's breath into Adam's nostrils, then the flow of rivers exiting Eden like in some movie, enhances the movement of the visual. Movement flow propels the narrative. And, as in dreams, physical movement moves us emotionally. If the reader, not inured to the repetition of the Genesis, permits oneself to experience the moving quality of creating the universe, we may approach Ezekiel's (perhaps more wondrous) heavenward journey, and his descent to tell us of this.

That is, we are placing both of Rambam's selections within the venue of moving visual experiences, not of quotidian reality (even such "realities" as Odysseus' ten-year journey home, or Abraham's journey to Canaan) but of a highly imaginative reality that approaches, even at moments exceeds dreams. Both Rambam and Freud were taken, grasped by the visual, moved by it emotionally; they took it as their challenge to transform the visual into words, preferably spoken words, in order to understand the visual more clearly, or at least to transmit it to another (one's self, one's fellow Jew, one's analyst).

The reader will not be surprised, as one thinks about one's own dreams, to learn that our visual cortex is perhaps tenfold larger than our auditory; that we show evidence of REM-sleep (visual dreaming) in infancy, long before we attain speech. We reflect on Aristotle's insight that on the stage, "spectacle," what is seen, is very powerful, despite Aristotle placing spectacle's "value" lower than the other criteria for poetry/tragedy. Maimonides in selecting these two remarkably visual events in *Tanach* and Freud in tackling his own visual haunting in dreams, then trying to transform and explain the visual into words, have tackled our more compelling ways of experiencing our worlds, particularly our hidden, chthonic words. As mentioned earlier in this book, Maimonides describes these two events—Creation and Chariot—as the two great secrets/contradictions (היסתיר, *histir*) in *Torah/Tanach*. He omits reference to one of the greater (if not greatest) secrets of the *Torah*, God's tetragrammaton name. For, a name is, after all, a sound, a voiced thing. It is not seen (although, per Moses, Isaiah, and Ezekiel, God was seen). For Freud, much of his decades' subsequent work was on the verbal in analysis, what was "said," with an occasional diversion into visual art, such as Michelangelo's *David*. But "spectacle," that emotionally charged visual that occurs against the dark sky of our nights, occurs with our eyes wide shut, is what propelled Freud into the deeper realms of his own life and consequently into ours.

Deaths, Loss, and Writing as Transformed Mourning

I return to remind the reader that both Maimonides and Freud wrote their significant works after being plunged into mourning due to the death of their beloved. For Maimonides at 39 years of age, this was the death of his brother David in 1177; for Freud, when he was 40, the death of his father (1896) initiated his studying dreams to understand his own suffering and resulted in the dream book. Later, his beloved elder daughter, Sophie, died in 1920 (at 27), then *her* three-year-old son, his grandson, when Freud was 64 and 67, respectively, after which he made the profound "turn" in his thinking articulated in the *Ego and the Id*.

How severe was Maimonides' reaction to his brother's death? Let's again listen to his own handwritten letter found in the Cairo *geniza*:

> *The greatest misfortune that has befallen me during my entire life—worse than anything else—was the demise of the saint, may his memory be blessed, who drowned in the Indian sea, …and left with me a little daughter and a widow. On the day I received that terrible news, I fell ill and remained in bed for almost a year, suffering from fever, despair and on the brink of destruction. Close to eight years have passed, and I still mourn for him for there can be no consolation. What can possibly comfort me? He grew up on my knees, he was my brother, he was my pupil…. My greatest joy was to see him. Now every joy has been dimmed. He has departed to his eternal life and left me confounded in a strange land.[7] Whenever I come across his handwriting on one of his books, my heart turns within me and my grief reawaken.*
>
> (Letters of Maimonides, Trans. Stitskin. 1977, p. 73)

He tells us a "misfortune worse than anything else," he confesses his bodily and psychic sufferings for a year, and he calls him, his David, "my student." The latter, let us keep in mind, is how he described the Joseph student, who later "left" prematurely and for whom Maimonides wrote the non-book, the *Guide*. He also more than hints, that he cannot console himself, what we today can understand in Freud's terms as melancholia, in which the shadow of the deceased falls upon one's own ego *(Mourning and Melancholia)*. Maimonides was 39 at this tragedy.

We recall for a moment King David's words/psalm over Jonathan's death, which Maimonides would have known well, given his encyclopedic knowledge of Scriptures:

> "…beloved and dear,/in their life and in their death, they were not parted, swifter than eagles, stronger than lions, …I grieve for you, my brother…."
>
> (9 Samuel, 2: 1: 23; Alter translation)

Maimonides, who began his medical practice in 1178, a year after David's death, worked on the *Guide* and delivered the first two books to his Hebrew translator in Provence in 1197, then the third in 1199, five years before his death. That is, during his medical practice, while he was the head of the Jewish community in Cairo and rabbi, and after he accepted his single student Joseph and upon Joseph's premature departure, he was working on this *Guide* (and perhaps his own perplexity). Maimonides would have been in his fifties.

We are suggesting that after the "loss" of his brother, then precious student Joseph, who also left prematurely, Maimonides transformed his mourning into a great work, the *Guide*.

The reader also knows that Freud admits that his father's death hit him profoundly, as Freud approached 40. Freud grasped his dreams, made sense of them in self-analysis (aided by letters to Fliess, which we suggest are like the "letters"—one of Maimonides' terms for the *Guide*—to Joseph), into one of his greatest works, the dream book. Both men made use of, and emerged from, their mourning by means of thinking critically and writing a book about deeper understandings.

Freud's second (and third) great losses were his eldest daughter's death, leaving behind two sons, one of whom Freud took in and was later "adopted" by Anna Freud.[8] The younger son, Heinele, died at three, leaving Freud further disconsolate. "Finding no enjoyment in life either" (Letter to Ernest Jones). *Nine years after Sophie's death*, trying to console his friend Binswanger who also suffered loss, Freud wrote:

> "...the acute sorrow we feel after such a loss will run its course, but also that we will remain inconsolable, and will never find a substitute....And that is how it should be. It is the only way of perpetuating a love that we do not want to abandon."
> (October 15, 1926, Freud letter to Binswanger)

Before Sophie's death, but affected by the slaughter of WWI—some 9–11 million soldiers alone; some 6–13 million citizens; some 23 million wounded (Wikipedia, 2022)—he wrote his *Mourning and Melancholia (1917*(. Then following her death, Freud began his *Ego and the Id* (1923), in which he drastically revises his ideas about inner life. We can suggest that the dream book is analogous to Maimonides' *Mishneh Torah*, and the *Ego and the Id* is more analogous to the *Guide*.

Or to grasp both men's most significant (in their eyes alone) works—the *Guide, the Interpretation of Dreams*—arose as they emerged from mourning. But, we will argue, their losses and mourning were preceded by significant *Bildung,* character development, that entails wide-ranging learning to build one's inner character. This term, *Bildung,* was thought to be characteristic of German/Austrian education from at least the nineteenth century

(Richards, 2022). In Freud's own gymnasium, not only Greek and Latin literature was taught (in their original tongues) but also Hebrew. Yet, as we have learned about Maimonides, he viewed a full education as one that entailed intimate familiarity with Tanach, Talmud, and also "physics" and "metaphysics," that is to say, Aristotle. Maimonides had *Bildung* centuries before the Enlightenment and Germanic "inventions."

There is significant psychoanalytic literature on how "creativity" can evolve from mourning. Pollock wrote:

> "I have studied …the impact of childhood …sibling… death on the creativity of Gustav Mahler, Edvard Munch, Kaethe Kollwitz, Thomas De Quinecey, Jack Kerouac, Bertha Pappenheim, Nietzsche, Goethe, Oscar Wilde, Lenin, Van Gogh, and Heinrich Schliemann,… (For) James Barrie, (of *Peter Pan*) the unexpected death of his brother affected the family, his life, and his creativity."
>
> (Pollock, 1986)

We do *not* argue that intimate death and subsequent mourning in and of themselves result in creativity. Rather, we suggest that at least for these two men, the *preceding inner build-up* of a solid (childhood) emotional life was combined with a deeply informed education. For, the early childhoods of both Maimonides and Freud were embedded in warm families, despite external vicissitudes (oppression by the Moors and exile for Maimonides; dislocation from a childhood home and early sibling loss for Freud). We know about Maimonides' education from his recommendations for other advanced students, and his own list of Neo-Aristotelian Arab philosophers complemented by his *Mishneh Torah*, in itself an extraordinary recounting of *Torah*, *Tanach*, and *Talmudic* knowledge. Freud's education was a hallmark of *Bildung*, including his *Torah* studies that he later downplayed (Grubrich-Simitis, op. cit.).

On this foundation, prior to the deaths of their beloveds, when the loss occurs of Maimonides' David, of Freud's father/Sophie/Heinele—the informed heart (Bettelheim, 1960) can reach within to explore the most hidden of secrets, to reveal the workings, the techniques of concealment of their own minds (via the *Torah* or the dream). And, neither turned to mystical accounts to explain the mysterious; they relied on reason informed by the heart. Maimonides would have referred to this as knowledge/wisdom infused with awe; Freud, the ego infused by libidinal powers at times fenced-in by superego constraints. That is, part of the successful working-through of mourning, to the degree feasible, included an almost ruthless (self)-examination, a questioning of received "wisdoms" (the literal interpretation of Torah, the literal interpretation of dreams), going against socially acceptable beliefs, jeopardizing their standing within their own communities, in order to seek out the more valuable hidden, the more meaningful, in order to elevate themselves out of the depths of mourning, and then go beyond, reach higher, to elevate their inner knowledge and lived lives.

In the Beginning Was Concealment (and Revelation)

Our fundamental premise in this book is that both Freud and Maimonides explored concealment and revelation (as performed by man in dreams, in writing). Halbertal's earlier book was entitled *Concealment and Revelation*. In it, he expands Leo Strauss's ideas about Maimonides (and Maimonides' ideas about the hidden/revealed of *Tanach*) by studying thirteen- and fourteenth-century Hebrew literature as exemplars of (Jewish) concealment and revelation. Strauss, in fact, put Maimonides on the *genre* of concealment/revelation, ranging from at least *Torah*, to Socrates' need to speak yet withhold, through Christ's parables, through the Gnostics and Judaic scholars who insisted on secrecy (*Hagiga*, for instance) on to Maimonides. Strauss points out that this genre proceeded at least until the eighteenth century, when, as Goethe lamented, this hidden style faded. But Strauss, a refugee from Nazism, an observer of fascist Communism (whether Russian or Chinese), demonstrated that the need for an author to hide his true meaning, coupled with the need to publish, continues the secret/revealed genre to the present. Strauss lists multiple motivations for a writer to hide: to protect himself (Galileo's mirror writing; Maimonides' parabolics, up to the Czech's Vaclav Havel's absurdist goading of the regime and to the present). But the writer also may feel the need to "protect" the naive or innocent (as Maimonides insisted), following Plato's suggestions of a noble lie in the Republic. (Or for different motivations, Churchill's (1991) "Bodyguard of lies" to protect his nation.)

By identifying Freud's genre as one of the hidden/revealed, we place his work in a two-millennia line of the genre of concealed and revealed; we place him on the continuum that Leo Strauss identified for us. In earlier work, we demonstrated that Rousseau's *Confessions* initiated the genre of autobiography in the contemporary sense (Szajnberg, 1992). Whereas Augustine's *Confessions* was premised on how Christ lured, enticed him *despite* his debauching childhood/adolescence/young adulthood, Montaigne's *Essays* articulated frank writing about his modest self, and Rousseau argued that his childhood (including his mother's death in childbirth, his father's later abandonment, and so on) *contributed* to the man he had become. Rousseau intended his book to be a version of concealment/revelation: he printed it privately for close friends to refute Voltaire's personal attack. The book was later pirated and sold publicly to Rousseau's dismay (Rousseau, 1781/1981; Szajnberg, 1992). Others continued this new genre of autobiography, more notably Goethe (Weintraub, 1974; Szajnberg, 1992). I argue in that paper that one can consider Freud's psychoanalytic technique as an oral-aural extension of autobiographic genre: in the dialogue—the analyst working almost as a compassionate editor to the analysand's "writing"—one hears the events of childhood and life as they influenced the later person. Bettelheim (personal communication, 1985) remarked that a good analysis goes through the following three phases:

> First, listen to how I was treated by my mother, father, sibling, and others.
>
> Second, this is how and why I suffer and have become who I am today.
>
> Third (and crucially), what is it I am doing to continue my internal misery. That is, what is the adaptive value for me to continue to live so maladaptively (Winnicott, 1974; Giovacchini, 2000).

The hiding, we may understand, at least as protective (protective from shame or guilt for one's self; protective from disapprobation or even attack from others). But what is remarkable—for Torah, Guide, and dreams—is both the desire to reveal *and* the techniques one can use to uncover the hidden. The desire to reveal we see in someone like Tycho Bråhe, who was burned to death for revealing his discovery of the universe, and in Galileo, who, even as he was threatened by the Church, kept writing, albeit in mirror script. Newton was different, it appears: when asked why he had not published his profound discoveries for years, until goaded by colleagues at the Royal Society, he remarked that he had already solved the problem for himself and saw little need to publish. Perhaps this may also have been true for Darwin, who did not publish his great species book until warned that he would be scooped.

But there is something different about so many others—authors of *Torah*, Christ's parables, Maimonides, that they appear compelled to embed hints to the enigmatic texts/narratives, for the "educated" to enlighten oneself.

A significant difference between Maimonides and Freud is that Maimonides sought to use techniques to hide; Freud did not do so. Like Enlightenment thinkers, Freud endeavored to reveal what was already hidden. Like William Harvey, who poked tubes into his vasculature to study circulation, Freud poked into his dream circulation to reveal truths not only about himself but ourselves.

What *is* remarkable, we hope we have shown, is not only that both Maimonides and Freud worked within the genre of hidden/revealed, but also that their techniques for hiding/revealing are remarkably, perhaps uncannily, similar. As shown in our chapters on *Guide* and dreams, both studied omission, contradiction, addition, and variations on these to unveil the hidden. What is different is that Maimonides admits that he will also use these same techniques to conceal his *Guide* text, to establish a labyrinth of roadblocks for the uninitiated. Freud did not do this. Or perhaps we might say, for Freud, one would need to have been initiated into an exploration of one's inner life to make use of Ariadne's thread to lead one through one's own and certainly other's labyrinthine dreams.

Uncannily similar? Perhaps not so uncanny, these mental mechanisms for embedding the gems within the dross. For, both men, although seven centuries separated, were dealing with matters of the mind. The *Torah,* whether written by God or God's emissaries, was written for mankind and was written to be "understood" by everyday mankind in order to live a proper life. Dreams too are dreamt by mankind. Well before Freud, dream interpreters (from Joseph on) believed there were hidden meanings within dreams, meanings that would better guide our lives. For Joseph, the Pharaoh's dreams—if understood and followed with proper actions—saved the Egyptians from seven years of famine. For Freud, our dreams, if understood to their fullest, will guide us to better grasping our present dilemmas, colored by our childhood past, and hence help us live better lives. Murray Wax, an anthropologist and psychoanalyst, argued that while mankind has made profound technological progress (writing, printing, railroads and cars, artificial intelligence, and Twitters), we remain mostly the same internally, we live the inner lives of our ancestral brain and impulses, and we continue to dream dreams that seem to make little sense (Wax, personal communication, 1998). We are not surprised nor find it uncanny that two men investigating our minds' needs and techniques to both hide and reveal secrets would discover similar mental mechanisms.

Stern's separate categorization of the parable in Maimonides' work, something slightly different from hiding and revealing, can also be applied to Freud's ideas of dream work. We recall that Stern identified Maimonides's use of parable as anything, even a single word, that tries to express what may be ultimately inexpressible because of our flesh, our desires, and needs. The human reaches for the Divine, he is tugged back to the moment by hunger, pain, exhaustion, or sexual fantasy. Or, brought back by sleep. "From dust to dust," we are and become. God curses Adam with this (Genesis 3:19), King Solomon notes the brief breath of life with this (Qohelet, 3:20), and Job despairs his fate with this (Job, 42:6).

Yet, in between birth and death, we have some aliveness, including, but not only, the aliveness that Maimonides encourages: to rise higher in our living. So too our dream states. Sleep may be considered transient forms of death from which we return. Children understand and may fear sleep, as they may fear their dreams when they begin to make sense of them as coming from within (Piaget). The Christian children's prayer captures a child's normative anxiety: "Now I lay me down to sleep, I pray the Lord my soul to keep./And if by chance I do not wake/I pray the Lord my soul to take." And the earliest recorded English use of the phrase "the little death" (1572) referred to sleep. Not until 1882 was it used as *"la petite mort"* for post-organic lassitude (OED, 2014, third edition).

We can consider dreams as a kind of parable, one we tell ourselves and don't "get" at first. But Stern clarifies: for Maimonides, as we discussed in the *Guide* chapter, some great truths we may never be able to attain and understand, precisely because we live in our "matter" (as Stern calls our bodies). Just so, Freud said that for dreams this is the navel that cannot be pursued any further for meaning. Just out of reach, some deeper truth, Maimonides and Freud tell us. For these areas that are deeply meaningful but just out of reach, parables are constructed. In Maimonides' sense, we can consider the dream as a form of parable, at least some parts of the dream. A story we tell ourselves in the hope that at least some meanings will be reachable by us, by one driven by passion for self-knowledge, schooled by Freud's techniques of uncovering.

We have journeyed some seven centuries, but traveled within the realm of that genre of the hidden and the revealed, an expanse of our (unknown) inner life.

It's a Jewish "book" the *Guide* Is. Why Study It?

This is Strauss's assessment and categorization (Strauss, op. cit.). Maimonides treats his *Guide* as written about *Torah*, as an antidote to perplexity for the Jewish student of Torah, Talmud, physics, and metaphysics. Why study it so intimately as we have asked you to do in the course of this book, unless you want to learn only about Jewish thinking?

But we almost say the same of Freud's dream book. It is written by a Jew, about dreams dreamt by a Jew (particularly Freud, but also many of Freud's early patients). Would we also call it only a book about Jewish matters? Freud feared that for his new discipline, psychoanalysis; hoped that the non-Jewish Messiah-in-the-wings, Jung, would save the discipline from categorization as a Jewish science.

But we learn from Freud not only about the content and meanings of his (Jewish) dreams and mind, but also about the mechanisms to understand the meanings of our own minds—Jewish or not.

So too, we argue, with Maimonides' *Guide*. Besides "learning" the meanings of two specific secrets of Torah—Creation and Chariot—we learn about the mechanisms of the mind as they create the genre of the hidden and revealed. We learn about the motivations for concealment and our cleverness of embedding hints to our deeper meanings within what is concealed. We learn how to discover the vein of precious gems within the bowels of our mental earth. There is, we argue, a line—at times continuous, at times discontinuous—from the *concealed/revealed genre* of *Torah*, through Socrates and Christ's parables, through Maimonides, to Freud's dreams.

But we could say that of Levi-Strauss studying Yanomami, how they sorted their camps alongside the river and how these arrangements reflected their marriage patters and social moieties. We could say that Levi-Strauss is learning something about the Yanomami; their camps are (unwittingly) organized by social and marital structure. But Levi-Strauss teaches us about humankind and how we have *unwitting* rules about social organization, even marriage. Galileo's study of dropping a feather and a stone from the Tower could tell us about a feather and stone, or about the generalized rules about gravity and acceleration; and Newton's observations from his beloved prism[9] could just tell us about ROYGBIV, the spectrum of colors that emerge, or about the physics of how light is composed, how it functions as a wave. That is, from the particular, the specific, if we think carefully, we may learn general scientific principles. From Freud's personal dreams, if carefully analyzed, we learn rules about dream formation; from Maimoinides' Torah and Guide, we learn principles about our mental mechanisms, such as the need to conceal precious messages, the techniques to conceal … and the inherent need to bury the secrets with hints to the dedicated, knowledgable student. The divide between the historical methodology of Voltaire versus Vico—study only the great moments of history versus the minute of any era (Berlin, 1998.)—is an artificial division. In fact, if we follow the minutiae with a thoughtful methodology, almost any era can become precious material. This is certainly true of analysis: the deep and long-term dedication to the minutiae, if done carefully, in a dedicated manner, not only reveals significant truths, but also moves one toward living a fuller life.

We profit by studying the intimate details of a fine thinker, as Vico suggested we study history: immersing ourselves. We profit from these two thinkers because by studying their thoughts in detail, we learn not simply (or even) about their inner lives, but also general principles about how we think and have thought in a veiled manner for centuries.

Our Fleshy Limits: Maimonides' Parable and Freud's Dream Navel

Our fleshy limits are explicated by Maimonides, something we at times will struggle against in our drive to more elevated belief and living. It is built in to our matter (Stern, 2013).

But Freud also dealt with the tension within our human nature, the tension between urges—aggressive, sexual—and our civilization from childhood. Early "Freudians" (not Freud himself), particularly those following Wilhelm Reich (or Carl Jung, whose sexual exploits with his psychotic patients marked at least his early career), believed that unleashing and acting upon our sexual fantasies would liberate, even "cure," us of our neurosis. They relied upon and distorted Freud's earlier writings. But *Civilization and Its Discontents*, a late work, 1930, captures the tension between fulfilling our desires versus the civilizing nature of childhood, a civilization that brings both blunting of our impulses (and possible neurosis) and living a more social existence into contention. The original title captures the book's nature: *"Das Unglück in der Kultur" or "The Unhappiness in Culturel*

Civilization" Unglück was altered to *Unbehagen*. Freud even suggested the English title *"Man's Discomfort in Civilization"* to his first English translator, Joan Riviere (and former analysand). Riviere chose *"Discontent." (see: Introduction to Civ. and its Discontents"* (Jones, Freud, 1930).[10] And Freud found that the "repression" that is part of becoming civilized is not simply from the outside world (parents and society), but rather there may be internal repressive forces. One can view Bowlby's (2008) ideas about attachment as a version of such internal forces: the inherent yearning and need for security and comforting that would "tame" our aggressive forces against those upon whom we depend. That is, out of concern for our protective caregiver (and for ourselves), we would self-tame destructive forces in favor of seeking closeness, safety, and comfort in (a providential) another (Searles and Flarsheim, 1974). We are suggesting an analogy between the yearning for a more noble existence that comes from within (not just God's demands) as what drives healthy seeking for greater knowledge; this yearning for our more noble spirit comes up against our fleshy limits, restraints on our knowledge thirst and seeking. We are Tower of Babels internatlly: yearning to reach upwards, then tumbled to the ground by the gravity of our physical selves. We make an analogy between Maimonides' implied or potential knowledge and awe-inspired seeking that *still* is limited by our flesh desires and needs and Freud's ideas about seeking self-knowledge (and the dependence that engenders attachment) that is limited by our impulses.

But —and this is a critical discovery about human nature—Freud transforms one feature of Maimonides' concern about the limits of our knowledge-seeking, our flesh needs. Freud suggests that we can harness at least some of our impulses—aggressive/assertive and sensual/sexual—in order to pursue more enriched lives. We do not have to remain embattled with our desires; rather we can harness them. He visualizes this when he gives the image of the charioteer—our ego—harnessed to two powerful steeds—id and superego—pulling in opposing directions. The charioteer's task is to decide on a goal, then to steer these often-opposing forces in the direction we decide upon. Intriguingly, unlike Ezekiel who is born aloft on a begemmed chariot, pulled by powerful four-winged beings with calves' soles, Freud puts us in the driver's position, standing poised, deciding how to direct our lives, and then harnessing the flesh-powered desires to our aim for a better life. Freud offers us hope in the genre of concealed/revealed. Not only can we learn what we have hidden from ourselves, but even within our human limits—that unplumbable navel—we can harness our impulses to build a better life.

We hope this book's exploration of both the concealed and revealed in Maimonides and Freud contribute to our understanding of how to build better, more enlightened lives.

Notes

1 With time and practice, Freud found other "roads" to the Ucs. and healing, such as symptoms, paraphrases, character flaws. And yet, dreams differ. We create our dreams and experience them, unlike symptoms and interpersonal relations. Dreams are our purest internal creations.

2 I use "*Torah*" even though the Chariot story is in the *Ketuvim* part of *Tanach*.

3 The tetragrammaton, "*Yehovah*," is only a word, not a visual experience, unlike the Creation and Chariot. "*Yehovah*" is in a different "class" of secret, although it too, the secret of this four-letter God name, one is prohibited from pursuing.

4 Breaths take seminal positions in the Genesis stories. *Ru'ach* riffles across the waters; *n'shimah* brings Adam to life, and later, *hevel*, Abel's name is also used in Qohelet, Ecclesiastes, and mistranslated as "vanity": instead, it means the shortness of a breath (Alter, op. cit.). That is, life, that interval between nothingness and death, is as brief as a breath of air. Also, *n'shima* (breath) is almost a homonym for *n'shama*, "soul."

5 Jean Piaget showed in his study of infants that they "believe" that they create movement by their own movement (Piaget, 1936).

6 This is the author's alternative to Alter's translation of *nefesh*.

7 "A strange land" brings to mind the Exodus verse of the Moses being a "stranger in a strange land" (Exodus 2:22). Moses names his first-born, "Gershom," which captures Moses' experience of being a stranger in this strange land of exile. His second son he named Ephraim, referring to Moses' "fruitfulness: (in this strange land).

8 This son, Ernest, continued to suffer from this early loss (Benveniste, 2015) despite great efforts by Freud and his family. Freud was in his sixties at this second loss and wrote to others how profoundly this wounded him (Benveniste, 2015). Ironically, Ernest was the toddler from whom Freud learned the "fort/da" spool game, in which the child tries to master the passive experience of being left by his mother in his room. We can speculate that from Ernst, Freud tried to learn how to actively cope with loss, now to change passive to active, in Freud's case, with the "thread" of reflection and writing. Freud, S. (1915) Letter from Sigmund Freud to Sándor Ferenczi, September 1, 1915. *The Correspondence of Sigmund Freud and Sándor Ferenczi*, Volume 2, 1914–1919 26:77.

9 Newton insisted that his portrait be painted with him cradling his beloved prism.

10 "The main theme of ("Civilization and Its Discontents")—(is) the irremediable antagonism between the demands of instinct and the restrictions of civilization—... Thus, on May 31, 1897, he wrote to Fliess that "incest is anti-social and civilization consists in a progressive renunciation of it" ... Nevertheless, in his early writings Freud does not seem to have regarded repression as being wholly due to external social influences. Though in his *Three Essays* (1905d) he spoke of"the inverse relation holding between civilization and the free development of sexuality" (*Standard Ed.*, 7, **242**), elsewhere in the same work he had the following comment to make on the dams against the sexual instinct that emerges during the latency period: '*One gets an impression from civilized children that the construction of these dams is a product of education, and no doubt education has much to do with it. But in reality this development is organically determined* and fixed by heredity, and it can occasionally occur without any help at all from education.' The notion of there being an "organic repression" paving the way to civilization—a notion that is expanded in the two long footnotes at the beginning and end of Chapter IV." (Italics added by this author) (Editor's Introduction, Civ. And Its Discontents).

References

Alter, R. (2019). *The Hebrew Bible.* Norton.

Benveniste, D. (2015). *The Interwoven Lives of Sigmund, Anna and W. Ernest Freud.* IPBooks.

Berlin, I. (1998). *The Proper Study of Mankind.* p. 334 ff. Pimlico.

Bettelheim, B. (1960). *The Informed Heart: Autonomy in a Mass Age.* Glencoe.

Bettelheim, B. (2010). *The Uses of Enchantment.* Vintage.

Borges, J. (2000). *This Craft of Verse.* Harvard.

Bowlby, J. (2008). *Attachment and Loss.* Vol. 1–3. Basic.

Churchill, W. (1991). *Memoirs of the Second World War.* Harper.

Freud, S. (1917). Mourning and Melancholia. *The Standard Edition of the Complete Psychological Works of Sigmund Freud*, 14:237–258.

Freud, S. (1923). The Ego and the Id. *The Standard Edition of the Complete Psychological Works of Sigmund Freud.* 19:1–66.

Freud, S. (1930). Civilization and Its Discontents. In: J. Strachey, Ed. *The Standard Edition of the Complete Psychological Works of Sigmund Freud*, Vol. 21, pp. 57–146. Hogarth Press.

Hirsch, E. (2006). https://www.poetryfoundation.org/articles/68417/mere-air-these-words-but-delicious-to-hear

Maimonides, M. (1977). *Letters of Maimonides.* Trans. L. Stitskin. Yeshiva U. Press.

Piaget, J. (1936). *Origins of Intelligence in the Child.* Routledge and Kegan Paul.

Pollock, G. H. (1986). Childhood Sibling Loss: A Family Tragedy. *Ann. of Psa*, 14:5.34

Rousseau, J. J. (1781/1981). *The Confessions.* Penguin.

Searles, H. and Flarsheim, A. (1974). Patient as Therapist to his Therapist and Commentary by Alfred Florsheim. In: Peter Giovacchini, Ed. *Tactics and Techniques Vol. II.* Aranson.

Stern, J. (2013). *The Matter and Form of Maimonides' Guide.* Harvard.

Szajnberg, N. (1992). Psychoanalysis as an Extension of Autobiography. *Int. Rev. Psychoanal.*, 19:375–378.

Szajnberg, N. (2013). Caravaggio: 400 years later, Psychoanalytic Portrait of his works. *J. Amer. Psychoanalytic Association.*

Weintraub, K. (1974). *Introduction to the Autobiography of Goethe.* University of Chicago Press.

Index

Note: Folios followed by "n" refer notes